D1603988

The North and Baltic Seas
The Mediterranean Sea
The Red and Arabian Seas
The Seas of China and Japan
The South Seas
The Caribbean Sea
The Sea Around Us

Dagmar Freuchen's
COOKBOOK
OF
THE SEVEN
SEAS

Dagmar Freuchen's
COOKBOOK
OF
THE SEVEN
SEAS

by *Dagmar Freuchen*

WITH

William Clifford

Drawings by Dagmar Freuchen

Published by *M. Evans and Company, Inc.*, *New York*

Contents

Preface

Peter Freuchen and I were introduced at a Christmas Eve dinner party in New York in 1944. Following his escape from a Nazi prison camp in occupied Denmark he had been working with the underground in Sweden, and the Danish government in exile had brought him here to lecture. I had emigrated from Denmark in 1938 and was drawing fashion illustrations for *Vogue* and *Harper's Bazaar*. The dinner, an old-fashioned Danish celebration with roast goose, rice pudding, and a Christmas tree, was given by Hans and Karen Bendix, who often invited stray, lonesome Danes on holidays. Peter had been asked to come for dinner at 7:30, but instead he arrived in the morning with two geese which he insisted on cooking himself. And when the time came he carved them with his pocket knife—the same one he had carried throughout the years in northern Greenland. For me it was love at first sight. And it was the same for him, as he recorded in his autobiography, *Vagrant Viking*:

"A few days before our party Hans told me that he had invited 'a widow by the name of Mueller' for Christmas and hoped I would have no objection. He gave me the impression that 'the widow' was some poor creature whom he wanted to treat at Christmastime. To my amazement . . . I could not help staring at her all evening, in fact I have a hard time still not doing so because 'the widow Mueller' became my wife Dagmar. She had been married to a Danish architect who had come to New York

7

to complete his studies. When the war broke out he had immediately volunteered, had been sent to the Pacific, and had never returned."

We got married the next year, but it was three years before we took our first trip to Denmark together. There I discovered how famous he really was. He was a national celebrity.

I suppose every Dane hears a little about Greenland and Arctic exploration, but I really knew next to nothing about the Arctic when we met. Peter, on the other hand, had actually lived the life of an Eskimo for many years. This was brought home to me one day soon after our marriage when I was struggling to open a can with a faulty can opener.

"My first wife," he remarked casually, "used to do that with her teeth." His first wife had been an Eskimo.

During our twelve years together (Peter died in Alaska on his way to the North Pole on an expedition, in 1957) he told me a lot about his life in Greenland and elsewhere. He had survived more than his share of physical trials, and he was brave but he was not pompous about it. "Arctic explorers are big actors," he wrote to Isak Dinesen in 1955.

Peter wrote lots of letters. He wrote them the first thing in the morning, to warm up, before beginning the day's work on his current novel or book about the Arctic or dispatch for a Danish newspaper. Every Sunday he wrote to his mother and to his sisters and other members of the family. He would write daily to anyone we knew who was in the hospital.

I think it is interesting that Peter turned to writing only after he lost a foot in Greenland. He had begun work there as an explorer and trader, but one time when he was out alone in a snowstorm he grew tired and stopped to rest. He was soon buried in the snow, and when it came time to dig himself out he discovered that he had left his knife behind on the sledge. An oversight like this can easily be fatal. Peter had a terrible struggle getting free of the ice, and by the time he was out one foot was frozen. Gangrene set in, and he knocked off a couple of toes himself, trying to stop it. Later the foot had to be amputated.

Assuming he wouldn't be able to get around so well any more (actually he still traveled a lot in later years), he turned to writing in place of exploration.

Among the many letters Peter wrote were congratulations to all members of his family and numerous friends on their birthdays. We also celebrated everyone's birthday by drinking hot chocolate in his honor. Danish children usually drink chocolate at birthday parties, and Peter continued that pleasure through adult life. He also formed a club for people who were born on his birthday, February 20th, which included Captain Carlsen of the "Flying Enterprise" and the young son of our friend K. Balaraman, correspondent of the Madras *Hindu* at the United Nations. Peter often said to me in the morning, "We have to drink hot chocolate this afternoon. It is so-and-so's birthday." He always drank it out of a mug. Peter collected mugs and was given new ones as Christmas and birthday presents.

Another ritual we always observed was the mustard eggs or "dirty eggs" on the Saturday before Easter. (The Danish name is *skidne aeg*.) These are eggs that have been boiled for about 8 minutes, shelled, and covered with a good thick mustard sauce. (The recipe is in Section One.) They are usually a lunch dish.

We often repeated the traditional Danish Christmas meal, served on Christmas Eve, consisting of roast goose stuffed with apples and prunes, red cabbage, and sugar-browned potatoes. Another traditional course is rice pudding with a hidden almond —just one almond hidden somewhere in the whole serving dish of pudding, and the lucky person who gets it wins a prize, usually a marzipan pig that has been on exhibition on the dining table throughout the meal.

Living in America, we naturally had roast turkey at Thanksgiving, but Peter did not like conventional bread stuffing. Often it isn't very good, and then he got too much of it when he was out on lecture tours, where he often spoke at lunch or dinner in a hotel, and the meal too often consisted of roast chicken or turkey with stuffing. We liked to stuff birds with parsley, grapes, shrimps, rice, and many other things.

Peter loved sweets and rich foods, perhaps partly because he didn't take any alcohol. When we went to restaurants he would usually study the dessert list first and decide how he was going to end the meal, then plan the rest of it accordingly. His favorite American dessert was apple pie. He ate lots of dried fruits and jam and candy—anything with sugar. He also loved chutney. Because he didn't drink, he often grew bored and hungry during the prolonged cocktail hours that came before dinner was served by many of the people who invited us. Then when we sat down at the table there might be another interminable wait while the host carved and stopped to talk. Peter would look at me, asking with his eyes why these people didn't have sense enough to do the basic carving ahead of time in the kitchen, and get on with the serving at a reasonable speed once we were sitting down and waiting.

Peter liked all kinds of fish and shellfish, usually cooked very simply. Plain boiled or steamed lobster, served hot with butter or cold with mayonnaise, was as good to his way of thinking as lobster with a fancy sauce. He thought cod was a noble fish—again simply boiled or poached. But it had to be very fresh. We sometimes bought from the fishermen in Connecticut, as Peter's mother had done at home in Denmark. When he was buying smelts or other fish for the cat he would get the fishermen to give him a couple of large codfish heads. People often bought steaks or fillets or even the whole fish without the head, but Peter knew the cheeks were a delicacy, and I recommend them to you if you have a cooperative fish merchant. Just boil or sauté them as you would a piece of codfish, allowing two or more per serving depending on size.

Peter used his pocket knife for everything, but always with a certain elegance. Although he had often eaten in the most primitive circumstances (and people who live where it is very cold, as in Greenland and Tibet, do not feel the same need for washing that we do), he always kept good table manners. He was surprised by the way most Americans eat fish, with only a fork, or with an ordinary dinner knife and fork. If we ate in a restaurant where they had no fish knives he asked for an extra fork and ate with one in each hand—a common practice in Denmark. I inherited a set of silver-bladed fish knives and matching forks, and only recently I gave a dinner with fish as the first course, setting the table with the fish knives and forks as well as dinner knives and forks for the main course. All of my guests used the fish fork but ignored the knife. And as we were all limiting our diets, I hadn't given them any bread to push with.

When I give a dinner party, like everybody else I try to do as much work as possible ahead of time. That way I don't have to worry about whether things will be ready on time, and I don't miss any of the conversation. Frequently I plan a whole dinner that can be fixed ahead, such as a recent one that began with pickled mushrooms as appetizers, marinated overnight in the refrigerator with a vinaigrette that included some garlic, paprika, and a drop of Tabasco. Then an aspic of shrimps in a ringmold with slices of hardboiled egg and chopped cooked carrot and celery, the gelatin flavored with clam juice, tomato juice, and cognac. I filled the center of the ring with green mayonnaise.

The main course was duck cooked with ginger and soy sauce, served whole on a platter with sliced red onions and oranges. I carved the breast in four lengthwise slices, and served them with green beans. The legs and wings were used the next day in salad. (I don't offer second helpings at a three-course meal.) Dessert was *coeur à la crème*, made of farmer's cheese surrounded with fresh strawberries.

In my cooking at home, and throughout this book, I try to follow ways of preparing good foods that are nonfattening. Peter was always working to keep his weight down during the years I was married to him, and most of my friends are on one sort of diet or another—low-calorie, low-carbohydrate, or low-cholesterol. I don't practice any terrible extremes, but I do believe that you can reduce the fat content of many dishes, sometimes to their advantage.

The need for a controlled diet is one of the good reasons for concentrating on fish, which gives you as much protein as meat, protein of the highest quality, with only about half the relative number of calories. But of course you have to cook it relatively simply and limit the amount of sauce. Peter and I usually steamed or boiled our fish (when I say boiled, I actually mean cooked in a small amount of water, not water to cover), and I generally follow the practice of cooking fat fish such as mackerel in court bouillon, while lean fish such as striped bass need only salted water. Incidentally with fish *meunière* if you serve several slices or wedges of lemon you can reduce the amount of butter.

If my cooking seems to be unduly influenced by Peter, the explanation is not only that he was a forceful man, but that I never had any interest in cooking until I married him. During my childhood in Denmark we had a cook at home. My mother didn't cook, and I never went into the kitchen. Women of my generation were supposed to be fully emancipated, and I gave all my time to my studies and to art. When I got married and came to America with my young architect husband I still put my career first. We never had a real kitchen, but used to take our meals at lunch counters or any sort of place that was quick and cheap. I'm sure our diet was poorly balanced, and it was poor in quality too. We sometimes got sick from what we ate.

Peter was interested in food, and for the first time I had a nice kitchen with adequate working facilities. Also we had a number of friends who had taken the Cordon Bleu course or were expert amateur cooks, and I caught the fever of competition. I began by getting some books. Now I have dozens of cookbooks, but only a couple of them concentrate on the sea, and only a couple take the whole world as their oyster. Putting together these two aspects of Peter's life and mine seemed to make a book.

For historical reasons everybody refers to the Seven Seas although as Peter observed it's easy to name fifty, and if you are talking about oceans it could be five, or perhaps better yet, one. For the continents are all islands in a single body of water. But the Seven Seas is a very old expression, dating from the time the Mediterranean peoples thought the world was mostly land. They identified just seven large seas, the other six besides the Mediterranean being the Red Sea, the Persian Gulf, the waters east and west of Africa, the Indian Ocean, and the China Sea.

For culinary purposes it also works out to group Peter's and my interests around seven different seas. The lucky number still serves its purpose, but some of the parts are new.

SECTION ONE. The North and Baltic Seas. This includes Denmark, where we both began, as well as the rest of Scandinavia and northern Europe including Russia. Because it belongs with Denmark in Peter's life, I've also put Greenland here.

SECTION TWO. The Mediterranean Sea. Not only southern Europe—France, Spain, Italy, and Greece—but the Mediterranean parts of North Africa and the Near East as well.

SECTION THREE. The Red and Arabian Seas. This area includes Arabia, East Africa, Pakistan, and India.

SECTION FOUR. The Seas of China and Japan. Besides the foods of the two major countries, this includes Korea and Vietnam.

SECTION FIVE. The South Seas. The whole vast, empty south Pacific, plus Australia and New Zealand, and the well-populated fringes of Southeast Asia.

SECTION SIX. The Caribbean Sea. All the islands, especially Puerto Rico, Haiti, and Jamaica. Also continental Latin America.

SECTION SEVEN. The Sea Around Us. Or *mare nostrum*, as the Romans called their own local waters. This is where I put the recipes that belong to our life in New York City, in Noank, Connecticut, or on Fire Island—the regional and international cooking of America, where Peter and I made our second home.

Perhaps I should emphasize that I haven't tried to write a comprehensive round-the-world cookbook, but only to present a selection of the recipes we liked best, as we prepared them at home and were served them by friends. For various reasons we always ate a great deal of fish, but this book is less than half a fish cookbook, containing many unusual recipes for meats, vegetables, and every sort of dish.

When I have a guest whose taste I'm not sure of, I usually avoid fish as the main course at dinner. Once in a while I slip up, but I always keep a couple of good cheeses on hand, and if a guest obviously isn't enjoying the fish, I bring them out quickly. A wedge of cheese, good bread, and a glass of wine, plus the vegetables, salad, and other parts of the dinner, never leaves anyone hungry.

I know that some great cooks are absolute purists in the kitchen, never using any prepared foods or short cuts. Others are not. Because I've always had a career—currently I teach fashion illustration at the Art Students' League—I adopt any time-saving conveniences that don't compromise quality. Sometimes I've tested a modern way of preparing a dish using packaged or processed ingredients side by side with the traditional and laborious way. I don't use many packaged foods, but the ones I do recommend are reliable.

*   *   *

Each section of this book has a brief Introduction, at the end of which I've listed a few sources for any unusual ingredients— things like hot green chili peppers, which I not only use in cooking but like to chew whenever I feel a cold coming on. Most ingredients are easy to find at any supermarket. If your supermarket doesn't have a good fish department, and if you live away from the coasts and the big cities, you may have a hard time getting fresh fish. But there's always frozen, canned, smoked, and dried fish. I've selected a number of recipes for the last section that work well with frozen fish (steaks or fillets, not fish sticks and breaded shrimps).

Brillat-Savarin wrote that the discovery of a new dish is more beneficial to humanity than the discovery of a new star. As we are on the verge of visiting new stars, I find it interesting that so many people are at the same time discovering and enjoying so much unusual food. I hope you will find many exciting new dishes among these recipes.

Dagmar Freuchen

SECTION ONE

The North and Baltic Seas

Introduction

ETER and I both grew up in Denmark, but we were a generation apart and his experience was much more traditional than mine. His father was a provincial shopkeeper who read Dickens aloud to the family every evening while his mother darned socks. Peter was the fourth of five children for the early part of his childhood, and then some years later two more younger sisters arrived. There were three maids, and it was a typical prosperous middle-class home. Or perhaps it was better than that, for Peter wrote: "We saw, to our constant amazement, that other children were afraid of their fathers. We loved ours. He loved us and he loved our mother. From this grew a happy childhood which we never forgot."

The eating and drinking habits were those of small-town Denmark of the time. Peter's father drank a cognac toddy each evening, made for him by his oldest daughter, with three pieces of sugar and warm water. A frequent visitor, a young bachelor jurist who befriended the children, was given a red wine toddy. Mother drank nothing, and it was completely unthinkable that the men might ever drink two toddies.

On Sundays, when the weather was good, there were picnics with baskets full of Denmark's incomparable open-faced sandwiches. The family often went in a rowboat, took friends along, and explored the sound. Once they rowed to a town where there was a restaurant, and instead of taking their food they bought a lunch of three fried eggs apiece, two pieces of fine bread with butter, and a large glass of milk. Peter felt overwhelmed by his father's generosity.

Ordinarily the family had its main meal at noon. In the afternoon there would be a big piece or two of rye bread for the children, spread with goose fat and sugar. They especially liked the heel of the loaf, but so did a boy named Alfred who worked in the store. The young clerks in the store were given food and drink, the latter consisting of Danish "white" beer, very low in alcohol. Altogether eighteen people were fed from the family kitchen, which kept one of the maids busy full time. (Another looked after the housekeeping, and the third took care of the children.)

Peter's mother did all the shopping, and some supplies came direct from the producers. Peter always remembered the distinctive taste of the milk supplied by the farmer who lived across the street (the last farmer to live in town). Straw and cow dung were filtered out of the milk after they got it home. Mother went to the butcher's and to several greengrocers and to a store for staples twice a week. Potatoes, flour, eggs, and even soup greens were bought directly from specialists in these items. Fish always came from the boats, and game was brought in to Father's store by the hunters. The family ate plenty of cod, except in months without an *r*, and pike, and flounder, and eel.

At six-o'clock supper each child got one piece of pure white bread, two pieces of light bread made from mixed white and rye flours, and as much dark rye as he could eat. There were cheese, pickled meat, chopped herring, chopped egg, meatballs, or cold roast to eat with the bread, and in season such things as radishes. But all these foods went only with the dark rye, except for cheese which one could put on the light bread. Nobody ever put anything on his single piece of fine white bread, and if occasionally a guest made this faux pas Peter thought he was a person "full of all the vices, and had not had parents to teach him correct habits and good manners." Forever afterwards in life he was unable to sink to the extravagance of putting anything on white bread without feeling guilty.

Mother and Father drank beer with their food, and Father also had a glass of aquavit "for his stomach." When there were thunderstorms, in summer, Father went to stand by at the fire house, the family drew the curtains (because lightning was known to come in through open windows), and one or two of the girls went to the kitchen to make "thunder coffee." Thunder coffee had to be particularly strong. The next morning everything would return to normal, and the children got their usual oatmeal, made from hard grain that had been cooked the night before. Sometimes it stayed warm all night, but often it had to be reheated and got burned. The taste of burned oatmeal porridge always brought back Peter's pleasant memories of childhood, but he virtually gave up oatmeal after having to eat it every day in a Nazi prison camp. I also have very strong memories of the oatmeal I ate in the hospital just after a minor operation. Is there some kind of a memory stimulant in oatmeal?

Breakfast oatmeal was ordinarily followed by nothing but dark rye bread with honey. However, on Sundays there was spiced zwieback or a roll or cinnamon bun fresh from the baker. And the household was always well supplied with homemade jam, Mother keeping her supplies a year ahead, in the old-fashioned way.

The butcher slaughtered two pigs a year for the family; the boys were taken to watch, but not the girls. When Peter's brother said it was too bad the pig had to be killed, their father explained that one must never pity animals about to die as that only toughened the animals' resistance and made it worse for them. When a pig was slaughtered mother made blood pudding, and Peter thought the blood pudding parties were the best of the year. "As a rule I ate myself sick," he wrote. Most of the pig went into the salt barrel, along with sausage and sometimes lamb.

A neighbor often gave the children dried fruits and cookies. In Peter's home, cookies were baked only at Christmas and Easter, but there was always a home-baked coffee ring to go with hot chocolate at birthdays. Altogether, living was not lavish but comfortable, very bourgeois, and shot through with the conservatism of a Danish (or any other) small town. The guiding principles seemed to be: behave yourself, don't do anything that might be questioned, avoid being talked about.

Peter decided to study medicine, but even before he entered the university he felt a strong yearning for adventure and a need to break away. On his seventeenth birthday he wrote to an uncle who had once gone off to Australia prospecting for gold: "I'd much rather go to sea at once and live as my grandfather did, having adventures like his. . . . Everything here at home is so certain and planned out that there's no chance for any risk or excitement. Often when I'm out sailing my boat I dream that it's going over unknown waters. . . . I think that the ones in my class who spend all day studying have less fun than I have when I go fishing. . . . I read in the papers that a student named Knud Rasmussen is on an expedition to Greenland with Mylius-Erichsen. It gives me something to think about. . . ." *

Being Peter, he didn't just think, he acted. Soon he and Knud Rasmussen became fast friends. They made many expeditions to Greenland together, founded and named the north Greenland settlement of Thule, and remained very close until Rasmussen's death in 1933. The anecdote Peter liked to tell best about their culinary experiences in Greenland related to a period when he and Knud had been eating nothing but musk ox for some weeks. Such a limited diet made them think and talk frequently about other foods, and one day they asked each other what they would choose if they could have absolutely anything at all to eat. After much reflection and careful consideration of the possibilities, each of them decided that his choice would be—more musk ox.

I haven't given any recipes for musk ox or other varieties of venison because these meats aren't generally available, but I have included a drink that Peter and Knud enjoyed countless times in

* from *The Peter Freuchen Reader. Messner, 1965.*

Greenland, and that we took to making at home in America. We called it Greenland Coffee or Coffee with Greenland Cream, and the idea is to make a cream substitute out of egg yolks. (There are no cows in Greenland, but plenty of birds.)

Peter had great love and respect for the Eskimos, whom he called "the most innocent, the happiest people I have ever known." He married a Greenland Eskimo, had two children, and became as integrated in Eskimo life as an outsider could be. He always did his best to adjust to their habits, though sometimes he was defeated by circumstances. For instance, he was not a good hunter, compared to most Eskimo men. He had never caught a narwhale from his kayak, and his wife had never been able to serve their guests the prized tail piece, a prime delicacy. Of course she could serve them tea and sugar and tobacco and other precious goods that Peter brought from Denmark, but these did not take the place of a tail piece from a narwhale caught by her husband.

Finally one day when a great party was planned in honor of his mother-in-law's visit, Peter had a chance to buy a narwhale from a friend. After the normal rituals of false modesty, protesting they had nothing fit to offer their guests, and so on, he brought in the beautiful tail. But the event was ruined by the wife of the hunter who had caught it saying she was glad they had found some use for *her* husband's whale.

In spite of or because of their hard life, Eskimos have a natural tolerance and helpfulness. They share their food with strangers, whether there is much or little of it, regarding a portion of it as the natural right of all human beings. The food and habits of eating are of course different from those of other men.

I've already mentioned the use of egg yolks with coffee. Another interesting Eskimo practice with eggs is to freeze them, raw. The whites become rather like ice crystals, while the yolks somewhat resemble fudge candy. You peel off the shells and eat them like apples, but they're something of a problem to handle unless you can eat them out of doors when it's below zero, because the white quickly begins to melt from the heat of your hand. I've sometimes wondered if they would fit into ice cream cones. Of course frozen eggs keep well through the winter in Greenland, and Peter frequently mentioned a cache of eider eggs as a particular delicacy. These duck eggs are almost twice the size of hen's eggs. Sometimes in June a dried egg-yolk sausage was made by removing all the white from fresh eggs and packing the yolks into a dried intestine of a seal. This is hung in the open air, though not in the direct sun, until it is thoroughly dry, sometimes all summer. Then it is cut into small pieces like candy.

Eskimos eat bear, whale, seal, walrus, musk ox, caribou, goose, duck, auk, and sometimes salmon or other fish that come their way. With the warming up of the northern waters that has taken place in our century, codfish are migrating farther north, while seals and walruses are retreating from the warmth. There is less and less of the traditional seal hunting in kayaks, creating basic changes in the old ways of life.

Besides the Eskimos, nobody I know of eats whale meat in any quantity except the Japanese, and I don't understand why, because the color and texture can be much like beef while the taste is similar to mackerel. Eskimos do not often catch the large white whales, unless they happen to surface right next to the kayak, but the narwhales were easy prey. Peter wrote about them: "Their skin—or *mattak*, as the Eskimos call it—is a great delicacy. It is cut out in large pieces, shiny and clean. The fat that sticks to the skin tastes like a rich, fresh juice while the outer skin has a delicious nutty flavor. The coarser inner skin is always swallowed without chewing and is supposed to give great strength. I have since learned that this *mattak* is rich in vitamins and provides effective protection against scurvy. It tastes like fresh vegetables and cool milk—all of Greenland concentrated in this tasty food. No man has ever been heard complaining or quarreling when the Eskimos gather around a fresh narwhale, tasting a piece of the delicate *mattak* before the flensing begins."* I had my first taste of *mattak* in 1956 when we went on a short trip to Iceland, where Peter was invited to lecture. We were given

* from *The Peter Freuchen Reader. Messner, 1965.*

24

a big cocktail party on the day we arrived, and one of the things they served was *mattak*, cut in half-inch cubes and skewered on toothpicks. I liked its taste, which reminded me of pickled watermelon rind. Recently I tasted it again in Montreal, at Expo 67, where it was called *muktuk*.

"When we cut up the whales we caught at Ugdli," Peter recorded, "we found that their stomachs were always filled with small Arctic flounders. We salvaged the fish and boiled it just as it came out of the narwhale. It tasted as if it had been prepared in a fine sharp sauce, and such a meal was so rare that we hardly dared to speak while we enjoyed it. Fish is, after all, practically nonexistent in Thule. Once or twice during the summer some old woman might catch a few, but no hunter with any self-respect would dream of fishing for something that volunteered to be caught and attached itself to a hook." *

I haven't included a recipe for boiled flounder with narwhale-stomach sauce for the same reason I don't give any whale recipes. I think these descriptions of Eskimo food are fascinating, but my book is not about this kind of cooking. Another time Peter reported that the skin of the white whale, when it was aged for a year and "in a thoroughly ripe condition," was a real delicacy. Apparently some meats benefited from ripening, but not all. Rotten bird meat was highly prized, whether eider duck or auk or ptarmigan. Well-fermented narwhale tail was food fit for an Eskimo orgy. But, as Peter described in *Vagrant Viking*, a rotten walrus quarter—delicious when it had decomposed just the right length of time—was nauseating when it went for more than a year. Peter and Knud Rasmussen served one of these to an American geologist who was trying to do them out of a meteor that had fallen in the Thule district. It was green and smelly from age, but Knud declined to serve anything else. "It would be a great pity to ruin this fine taste by coffee," he said.

"You must finish the meal in true Eskimo fashion. The taste is supposed to stay with you."

---

* from *The Peter Freuchen Reader. Messner, 1965.*

25

At an Eskimo banquet frozen raw meat comes first, usually followed by cooked walrus or seal. In some societies boiled meat is considered man's food exclusively, too good for women to eat. The meat is boiled plain, forked up in chunks, and eaten with cups of the bouillon, which is likely to be a thick fat-covered blood soup. Peter compared it to hot chocolate. Soup from boiled bear meat is strong and spicy. Bear liver is sometimes made into a ragout, but the Eskimos generally avoid it, knowing it can be poisonous. Their dogs seem to know when to eat it and when to leave it alone.

An Eskimo wife may not actually eat such a luxury as boiled meat herself, but she is allowed to help her husband and his guests get started. She lifts the chunk of meat out of the pot with a fork made of caribou antler or walrus rib and licks it dry, to prevent soup and blood from dripping too much on the men. Then she passes it to her husband, who takes it in his hands and puts a corner of it in his mouth. With his knife he cuts off the re-

mainder and passes it on to a guest. He in turn does the same, and the chunk of meat passes around the circle of guests until it is gone, when it is replaced by another. From time to time a piece of blubber is passed around in the same way. A certain amount of blood gets smeared over hands and face, and when a piece of meat falls on the floor the man who picks it up is always polite enough to lick it clean. Cooking pots are not washed, but only wiped off with a piece of skin once a month. This was the life of the Hudson Bay Eskimos. The Thule Eskimos were more chivalrous (i.e., their women were allowed to eat more cooked meat), and they kept their cooking pots relatively clean.

Peter was invited to taste many strange dishes. He described the gourmet preparation of a duck as follows:

"Take a female duck, pluck all the feathers and down off, then skin the bird to the neck. The meat [i.e., the carcass] is added to the pot [to cook in a soup], but the skin is tied around the neck to form a closed bag which is dropped in the boiling water. The fat inside the skin melts and the skin bag itself swells so it looks as if it were stuffed to capacity. When it is finished, the cook opens it by unwrapping the string around the neck, and then the liquid fat pours out when she presses the skin. Children and closest friends are invited to get some of the hot fat by sucking it from the skin through the neck. And when the skin is entirely emptied it is eaten with great relish." *

I admit that I have never been tempted to prepare any of these dishes at home, nor do I suppose you will want to. I am told that even Eskimo habits are changing nowadays. When Peter returned to Greenland in 1951 he was served such luxuries as bread, butter, and bacon—imported ingredients that he had learned to do without in his earlier years. And beef, pork, fruits, cheese, pastries, canned goods of every sort. Finally he was offered one Eskimo dish, reindeer. He wrote to me about eating this reindeer while I was doing some work in Paris: "You are dining in Paris at the same time—life is full of variety." Other people often commented on the contrast between his primitive life with the Eskimos and my work in high fashion. At this time I was making many drawings for *Vogue*, and Irving Penn took a photo of us— Peter in Arctic fur coat, me in basic black—that made the point.

* from *The Arctic Year. Putnam, 1958.*

But some habits resist change. The cook at the Greenland guesthouse in 1951 boiled the reindeer meat and the men drank the soup. Then when they asked her to wash the table she did it with some of the leftover soup, explaining that it would make the table smell good. Peter was surprised to find a large modern bakery there making Danish pastry, and beer was being brewed. He wrote me, "I often have to give up talking to people because they are drunk."

During his early years in the Arctic Peter returned from time to time to Denmark, and after his first wife died he bought a small island with a farm and settled there. Of course he was only relatively settled, for there were always lecture tours—throughout Scandinavia, to England, Germany, and America—and international conferences, and further exploring expeditions, and visits to Hollywood and various other places for movie-making. The Denmark to which Peter returned was the more modern place in which I grew up. Still, as with the Eskimos, certain traditions resisted change, especially where food was concerned.

In my family we had the custom of everyone choosing his favorite dishes for his birthday. On my father's birthday, December 9th, we always began with oysters on the half shell, then had either venison or roast duck, and caramel pudding for dessert. For my birthday I chose little pastry *croustades* filled with creamed chopped ham and vegetables, followed by roast veal. And always, for dessert, meringues filled with whipped cream Danish *Hofdessert*—the recipe is in this section).

As a small child I was skinny, but from the age of about twelve to fifteen I was overweight. And no wonder, with all the whipped cream and butter and other riches in Denmark. Every day on my way home from school I stopped at a bakery with one or two girl friends and we bought some pastry, either macaroon cake or butter cake, which we gobbled down on the spot. Sometimes we even sat down at a table—pastry shops in most parts of Europe have a few tables to accommodate people whose sweet tooth gets the better of them—and ate layer cake. My favorite was one called Othello cake, with chocolate frosting.

My best friend in school was Grete Mueller, whose cousin Torben became my first husband. Grete introduced us; she loved to bring people together and was always arranging parties, although she never had any money to spend on them. The first of her many parties I remember was at her parents' house when we were still in our very early teens. Her father was a civil servant, and there were eleven brothers and sisters (with Grete somewhere in the middle) and no servants. But each of the children was able to do something useful for the whole family. I remember one of the boys knew how to repair shoes.

Because everybody in their family did something, I was put to work too. On this particular occasion (which I will never forget) I was asked to bake a *Galopkringle* for the party. It is a kind of Danish pastry with almonds, raisins, and candied lemon or orange rind. The dough is shaped like a giant pretzel, then sprinkled with sugar and spices before baking. I had never before done anything at all in the kitchen, so this was quite a challenge and I was flattered that they trusted me with it. Somewhat to my surprise, the *Galopkringle* came out fine.

I didn't go into the kitchen at home because, as a modern girl, I was supposed to be freed of such drudgery. Also our family cook, Marie Olesen, was a tyrant who was better left alone to manage things in her own way. Sometimes when we had company coming for dinner she would ask who it was so that she could decide if the guests were worth a real effort on her part. Her real efforts could be most impressive—fine French sauces, and elaborate show-pieces, though she tended to be careless about everyday things like boiled eggs. She ran my mother's kitchen, and to some extent our lives, for thirty-five years, at the same time acting as an emergency veterinary when there were any sick domestic animals in the neighborhood.

Every July during my childhood we closed our house near Copenhagen for two weeks and went to a resort hotel on the seacoast. Both the cook and the maid went on vacation during these two weeks. The rest of the year each of them had a weekly day off, and on cook's day off, the maid usually reheated something the cook had prepared ahead. Or the maid herself might cook us something simple such as pork tenderloin, a very popular dish in Denmark. I've often wished I could get pork tenderloin more easily in America, but few butchers seem to have it. (They tend to cut their pork chops across the loin, instead of removing the whole loin to sell separately.) It can be sliced and pan-broiled like a steak or chops. Whole, it can be roasted, pot roasted, or braised. It's very good stuffed, either with parsley or with prunes. If you can get the whole loin, I urge you to try it this way.

Once we had a temporary substitute for Miss Olesen who was also a good cook. I remember that she wore very elegant clothes on her day off, when she went out with a fiancé who worked in a licorice factory. I thought he was wonderful. Once when she hadn't finished her work in the kitchen and kept him waiting a long time in her room, he got bored and turned all the pictures upside down.

The father of another of my classmates was the Danish importer of Swiss chocolate, and I thought he was just as wonderful as the temporary cook's fiancé. In their home were large sample boxes with rows and rows of little rectangular chocolates, each row in a different colorful wrapping. The Danes eat a lot of chocolate candy, but Danish children don't eat so much ice cream or drink so many soft drinks as children in America. (At least they didn't, the last I knew.)

Recipes for the specialties of Danish cooking that Peter and I both liked best are given in this first section, together with a selection of other dishes from countries of northern Europe, stretching as far east as Russia. Peter visited Russia as a guest of the state in the late 1930's and while a great many things went wrong, he was very pleased with the good tea and wonderful jam. The meals he was served were old-fashioned in their abundance, and he took to drinking the Russian beer, *kvas*, although normally he didn't drink anything alcoholic. (He had also once accepted a glass of champagne from the King of Denmark, with no great enthusiasm.)

While the Eskimos may have scorned anything from the sea that was easy to catch, the Danes enjoy just about every well-known fish and shellfish, and they cook them all well. Among the major ones are cod and such members of its family as haddock, hake, and whiting; salmon; sardines; herring; and among the flatfish halibut, plaice, sole and flounder. Oysters, mussels, crabs, and lobsters are all popular. Many of these fish appear both fresh and salted, pickled, or smoked.

Although Peter was exposed to great hardship and suffering in Greenland, it didn't harden him to the point where he could accept deliberate cruelty toward men or animals. When he found out how geese were force-fed to swell up their livers and produce the material for fine goose-liver pâté, he wrote so much about this cruel treatment in the newspapers that he finally succeeded in having the force-feeding of geese prohibited in Denmark. He still liked pâté made from pork and chicken livers.

One final comment on Danish cooking: practically every dish is served with a sauce. Danes make all the basic French sauces, white and brown, hot and cold, and use them relentlessly. They can make dozens of béchamel variations to serve with fish. They also mix in lots of whipped cream, and horseradish, and they put fruit in brown sauces. There's no written rule, but the feeling is that to please the Danes, food must have a sauce. One time Peter and I went to a reception at the United Nations, one of the large receptions that take place frequently while the General Assembly is in session where all nationalities are present. Sometimes the food is rather fancy at these affairs, but this one happened to be very plain. And there wasn't a single fellow Dane in sight. Finally we saw one man we knew and asked him, "Where are all the Danes?"

"They're sitting together over in the corner, sulking," he replied. And he gestured at the buffet table, "See, no sauce."

Open-Faced Sandwiches
(Smørrebrød)

Danish *smørrebrød* (literally "buttered bread") isn't the same thing at all as the Swedish buffet table called smorgasbord. It's lighter (you have it for lunch or late-evening snack, never dinner), and I think prettier, and while it resembles sandwiches, you have to eat with a knife and fork. Every visitor to Denmark is impressed by *smørrebrød*. It is the basis of most Danish lunches, whether eaten at home, at a restaurant, in school, in the office, on a picnic, or any other place. And the restaurants employ skilled specialists called *smørrebrødsjomfruer* who turn out big quantities of fancy ones at high speed. The *smørrebrød* produced at home is seldom as spectacular-looking as the kinds made in restaurants, but it tastes as good. Anybody with a little sense for decoration can do it, and I think that *smørrebrød* is fun for do-it-yourself buffet meals. But once your guests have assembled the materials from the buffet, they have to have tables where they can sit down and eat with knife and fork. I think it would be difficult, if not impossible, to eat *smørrebrød* from just a plate or a tray on one's lap.

Here are some pointers and specific suggestions for making *smørrebrød*. The *brød* (bread) has to be very firm, whether you choose white, rye, or pumpernickel. Crackers, toast, and flat breads from Scandinavia should not be used because they will get soggy. Keep them for cheese or other *smørrebrød* that you prepare and then eat immediately. The *smør* (butter) should be the freshest and best you can buy, preferably sweet butter, served at room temperature. Spread it about $\frac{1}{16}$ inch thick over the whole piece of bread. Many Danes would spread it $\frac{1}{8}$ inch thick, but I think that's too much—although I admit Danish butter is so good it's hard to get enough of it.

The main ingredient or covering of the bread is called the *paalaeg*. Various canned fish make good *paalaeg*, and here are a few of my favorites:

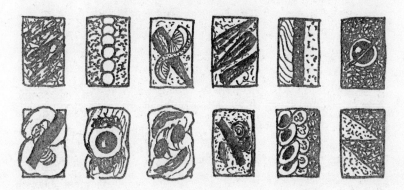

Pickled herring on pumpernickel (always of course with butter), decorated with a little fresh dill.

Chopped smoked herring and chopped hardcooked egg mixed together, decorated with a row of radish slices down the middle.

1 or 2 skinless and boneless sardines on a bed of shredded lettuce with a ½ inch row of chopped hardcooked egg at the side and a wedge of lemon to squeeze.

½ inch covering of cold scrambled egg topped with 3 or 4 small Brisling sardines in tomato sauce.

Strips of smoked salmon, cold scrambled egg, and chopped cooked spinach (hot or cold) side by side.

Paalaeg of meat very often use up leftover roast meats, but first I'll give my favorite meat *smørrebrød*, which is a delicate and delicious steak tartare. We used to call this *løvebøf* (lion-steak), and it always made us feel strong and fierce. Cover the buttered bread with a layer of scraped raw sirloin at least ¼ inch thick. Make a slight indentation in the middle and fill it with a whole raw egg yolk. Cut a raw onion ring to fit around the egg yolk, and cross the top of the yolk with a single anchovy fillet (like the ribbon of honor across the chest of a French diplomat). Decorate the plate with small mounds of capers and shaved fresh horseradish.

Sliced roast veal topped with a slice of meat aspic and a bit of cucumber salad.

33

Sliced roast beef, fried onions, and a cold fried egg on top.

Sliced roast pork with a piece of crackling, garnished with prunes or slices of apple, or both.

Liver pâté is used more than any other *paalaeg*. It is put on thick and topped with a slice of aspic, a slice of pickled cucumber, or pickled beet. But not too much of the pickles—the pâté should never be soaked.

Slices of hardcooked egg, cucumbers, or tomatoes make good *smørrebrød*, especially when topped with baby watercress.

Sometimes Danes serve *snitter*, which are half-size *smørrebrød* or smaller, like canapés. This is the way you can adapt *smørrebrød* for use with cocktails as a first course at a dinner party. They're also good with beer, or with afternoon tea or coffee. My mother served *snitter* when she had friends in to play bridge. There is one kind she served that I sometimes make today. Cut buttered bread in triangles. Separate hardcooked egg whites and yolks, and grate separately. Mix as much horseradish as you like with sour cream, mix in egg whites, and top half the triangles with this. Mix mustard to taste with mayonnaise, add yolks, and top the other half of the triangles with this. Arrange triangles on plate or platter to form a kind of checkerboard.

This is only a tiny sampling of the hundreds of Danish *smørrebrød*, but I hope these few models will help you to make your own from whatever ingredients you happen to have.

Cherry Soup
(Sødsuppe)

Fruit soups are very popular in Denmark, and this recipe can be varied by using elderberries, blueberries, gooseberries, rose hips, or even rhubarb. If you don't like such a sweet first course, you can eat it cold, as a dessert, with sweetened whipped cream.

3 cups sour cherries, pitted   ½ cup sugar
6 cups water   1 tablespoon cornstarch
Grated rind of 1 lemon   Zwieback
2 tablespoons lemon juice

Cook 2 cups of the cherries in the water with lemon rind until they become very soft. Put in blender until smooth. Add the remaining cup of raw cherries, lemon juice, and ½ cup sugar, or more to taste. Thicken with cornstarch and serve hot, garnished with bite-sized pieces of zwieback. *Makes 6 servings.*

Beer Soup
(Øllebrød)

This soup is just as good made with beer that has been left open for some time and gone flat. And some people prefer it with dark beer.

> 8 *slices (about 10 ounces) Danish rye, pumpernickel, or any*
>   *heavy dark bread*
> 3 *cups beer or ale* (2 12-ounce bottles)
> 2 *cups water*
> *Grated rind of 1 lemon*
> *Sugar*
> *Whipped cream (unsweetened)*

Break up bread and put it to soak in beer and water overnight, or for at least 2 hours in a warm kitchen.

Bring to boil, add lemon rind, and simmer uncovered for 15 minutes. Put in blender until smooth, return to heat, and add sugar to taste. Heat through but do not boil. Garnish each plate with a spoonful or two of whipped cream. In Denmark, children sometimes get as many spoonfuls of cream as they are years old. *Makes 4 servings.*

Chervil Soup with Poached Eggs

Fresh chervil is rarely available in the markets, but you can grow it in your garden. This recipe also works with an equal amount of fresh watercress or spinach, or with half the quantity of dried chervil, although the results will be different in each case.

4 cups meat or chicken stock
1 tablespoon potato flour or cornstarch
4 tablespoons finely chopped fresh chervil
4 poached eggs
2 teaspoons chopped chives

Heat the stock to boiling point and thicken it with flour mixed with a little cold stock or water. If stock has not yet been fully seasoned, add salt and pepper to taste. Add chervil and heat through, but do not allow to boil. Put a poached egg in each of four soup bowls and pour soup over it. Garnish with chives. *Makes 4 servings.*

Cream of Cucumber Soup with Dill

This is my favorite summer soup, very refreshing and easy to make in an electric blender.

4 medium cucumbers
4 cups chicken bouillon
1 tablespoon cornstarch
1 cup cream, or half-and-
   half

Pinch of cayenne pepper
4 tablespoons chopped
   fresh dill, or 2 tablespoons dried dill

Peel cucumbers, cut in half lengthwise, and remove seeds. Chop coarsely and cook in bouillon until soft. Pour into blender and blend until smooth. Pour back into pan and bring to boil. Dissolve cornstarch in 2 tablespoons cold water, add to pan, reduce heat and simmer a few minutes, stirring frequently. Allow to cool. Add cream, cayenne pepper, and dill, then chill well. Serve ice-cold in chilled cups. *Makes 6 servings.*

Lobster Soup
(Hummersuppe)

2 1-pound lobsters, or 1 can
(6½ ounces) lobster
meat
6 tablespoons medium
sherry
1 carrot
1 small onion

4 tablespoons butter
2 tablespoons flour
1½ cups milk
1 cup cream
2 egg yolks
Salt and pepper

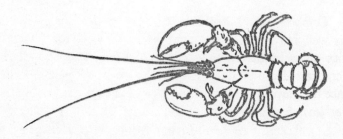

Wash lobsters and steam them for 10 minutes in 1 cup salted water. (If weight of lobsters runs over 2 pounds, steam for 5 minutes per pound.) Remove lobster meat from shell and dice, saving any liquid that runs out of shells. Put diced meat, tomalley (the soft green substance, which is the lobster's liver), and any coral or roe to marinate in the sherry for ½ hour. Crush shells, place in water in which lobsters were steamed, add liquid saved from cutting up lobsters, together with cut carrot and onion, and cook for 20 minutes. Strain. Use this lobster stock in making white sauce. (If you refuse to fuss with live lobsters, look for a container of fresh lobster meat at your fish store, or substitute a can of lobster meat, and use canned clam juice for the stock.) Make a white sauce of the butter, flour, milk, and lobster stock. Add cream and beat in egg yolks, being careful not to boil. Add lobster with sherry, salt and pepper to taste, and simmer very gently for 10 minutes. *Makes 4 servings.*

Sardine Spread

2 3½-ounce cans of sar-
   dines, mashed
2 tablespoons lemon juice
1 cup whipped cream
   cheese
2 tablespoons chopped
   parsley

Salt and pepper
Strips of green pepper or
   cucumber boats
Chopped radishes or
   pimento

Combine first 4 ingredients with salt and pepper to taste. Mix well and refrigerate at least 1 hour. Serve on green pepper strips or cucumber boats with seeds hollowed out (or on toast or crackers if you prefer). The taste is good but the color dreary, hence the garnish of chopped radish or pimento. *Makes 1½ cups or at least 6 appetizer servings.*

Cod Roe Pâté

Several brands and various sized cans of cooked cod roe from Scandinavia are sold in delicatessens and gourmet food stores. It can be sliced and sautéed, just as you would cook canned shad roe. I also like to make this pâté out of it, to serve with cocktails.

½ pound canned cod roe
1 teaspoon anchovy paste
6 tablespoons butter

2 tablespoons ketchup, or
   to taste

If there is any membrane on roe, remove and discard. Beat ingredients until well blended, pack into mold, and chill. Turn out on lettuce leaf, surround with lemon wedges, and serve with crackers or triangles of dark bread. *Makes about 1½ cups or at least 6 appetizer servings.*

Pickled Salmon
(*Gravlaks*)

Maybe this raw pickled salmon is even better than smoked salmon. It looks somewhat the same, and is mostly served the same way, but it really tastes quite different. The last time I was in Sweden I kept ordering it at every restaurant even though it was one of the most expensive items on the menu. Fortunately for my bank account, it isn't too difficult to make at home. The main requirement is a large piece of really fresh spring or summer salmon, not frozen fish.

1 *4-pound section of salmon, preferably middle cut*
3 *tablespoons salt*
1 *teaspoon white peppercorns, crushed*

3 *tablespoons sugar*
3 *bunches fresh dill*
Twigs of pine or spruce, if available
2 *tablespoons cognac*
1 *lemon, cut in wedges*

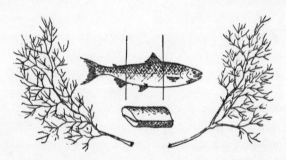

Bone the fish and separate it carefully into two sections or fillets. Do not scrape or rinse, but dry with towel. Mix together salt, pepper and sugar, and sprinkle mixture on boned (flesh) sides of both pieces. Spread half of the twigs and 1 bunch of dill on the bottom of a deep flat dish, and place one of the pieces of fish on this bed, skin side down. Spread another bunch of dill over fish, sprinkle on cognac, and place second piece of fish on it, skin side up. Turn fish to make the most compact "sandwich," putting the thin end of one piece over the thick end of the other. Cover with remaining dill and twigs, and put a board or plate with a weight on top. Keep in cool pantry or bottom of refrigerator for 36 hours. Scrape off spices and slice thin like smoked salmon or in regular serving pieces. Garnish with fresh dill and wedges of lemon, and serve with any mustard sauce or a sweetened mustard vinaigrette. *Gravlaks* will keep a week in the refrigerator. *Makes 12 or more servings.*

Stuffed Mushrooms

Use medium-large mushrooms, 1½ to 2″ in diameter, as firm and fresh as you can find. The pâté can be either homemade or commercial. I often use a canned pâté from Denmark that has bits of truffle in it.

12 mushroom caps	1 tablespoon minced parsley
4 ounces liver pâté	ley
1 tablespoon cognac	1 tablespoon heavy cream

Clean mushroom caps but do not peel. Mix cognac and parsley into liver pâté, then mix in the cream a teaspoonful at a time. You don't want the mixture to become soupy, and if you are using a very creamy pâté you may not need the whole tablespoonful of cream. Fill mushroom caps with mixture, piling it up high. Arrange on a buttered dish and bake in a 325° oven for 12 minutes. If you want the mushrooms to cook faster, you can first sauté the caps in a little hot butter, then stuff, and put in the broiler for about 6 minutes. Serve warm but not burning hot. *Makes 6 appetizer servings.*

Herring Salad
(Sildesalat)

I've sometimes wondered why herring salad isn't popular here in America. We do eat lots of salads, and this fuchsia-pink one is such an attractive variation. Traditional herring salad has potatoes and a boiled dressing, where my version uses hardboiled eggs and sour cream (or half sour cream, half yogurt, if you want to cut calories). I make it like this both for convenience and to reduce carbohydrates. The quantities of the ingredients can be varied to taste, but always use as little dressing as possible —just enough to bind the ingredients together. This salad can be used for canapés or sandwiches, in which case you should cut the ingredients somewhat finer than for serving as salad. When I was a child I discovered one other use for herring salad. During the lunch period one day at school a boy started doing something that made me angry (I don't remember what it was), and I took an open-faced herring salad sandwich out of my lunch box and hurled it smack in his face. Beets being the color they are, his whole face turned purple.

1 *salt herring, or a 7½-ounce jar of pickled herring*
½ *cup diced pickled beets*
½ *cup diced tart raw apples*
2 *tablespoons chopped raw onion*
2 *tablespoons chopped cucumber pickle*
4 *hardboiled eggs, chopped*
½ *cup leftover cooked ham or veal (optional)*
½ *cup sour cream (or half sour cream, half yogurt)*
2 *tablespoons beet juice, or more for depth of color desired*
Salt, pepper, mustard, sugar

Soak salt herring overnight in cold water, drain, discard skin and bones, and chop. Or drain jar of pickled herring and chop. Add beets, apples, onion, cucumber pickle, and half of the eggs. You can also add ½ cup of leftover cooked ham or veal. Mix together the sour cream, beet juice, and a pinch of each of the seasonings, or more to taste. Add all chopped ingredients to dressing and mix. Rinse a mold or bowl with cold water, pack salad into it, and refrigerate. Just before serving, turn out of mold and decorate with remaining egg. *Makes 4 salad servings.*

Marinated Roast Green Peppers

A friend who grew up in Baku, on the Caspian Sea, gave me this simple recipe for a delectable hors d'oeuvre. I like to begin dinner with a first course like this, not heavy, and something you can fix well in advance.

4 *green peppers*   *Salt and pepper to taste*
3 *tablespoons olive oil*   *Pinch of Coleman's mus-*
1 *tablespoon wine vinegar*   *tard*

Scald the peppers, then bake them whole, unseeded in a 350° oven for 1 hour. Peel if desired (not absolutely necessary), cut into quarters, and discard the seeds. Combine other ingredients (or make your own preferred vinaigrette), pour over the peppers, and marinate in the refrigerator overnight. Serve chilled. *Makes 4 servings.*

Poor Man's Caviar

This eggplant appetizer is another dish from the Caspian, though something like it is made almost everywhere eggplants and oil are available. Eggplant seems to absorb almost any amount of oil you allow it to, but a poor man can't afford gallons of oil, and neither can a rich man who wants to keep his figure.

1 large eggplant
1 large onion, diced
1 large green pepper, diced
¼ cup olive oil

1 teaspoon salt
¼ teaspoon pepper
2 tablespoons lemon juice

Roast the eggplant, whole, in a 400° oven until it is soft. Peel and chop the pulp. Squeeze out or drain excess liquid. Sauté the onion and pepper in oil until soft. Add eggplant, salt, and pepper, and continue to sauté until well blended and cooked. (This method of cooking the eggplant first without oil gives a better result with less oil than if the raw eggplant is sautéed with the onion and pepper.) Add lemon juice and chill. Serve ice cold with toast. You can vary the taste by leaving out the green pepper, adding tomatoes, garlic, etc. *Makes 4 servings.*

Liver Pâté
(*Leverpostej*)

It's easy to make liver pâté, and this one tastes much better than most of the ones you can buy ready-made. In Denmark there are many variations and recipes, but this is a standard and popular one.

1½ pounds pork liver	1½ cups milk
½ pound pork fat	2 eggs, beaten
1 onion	2 anchovies, minced
3 tablespoons butter	1 teaspoon pepper
3 tablespoons flour	

Grind liver, pork fat, and onion twice, each separately. Make a white sauce with the butter, flour, and milk, cooking until smooth and thick. Add the fat and the onion and cook until fat has melted, stirring constantly. Remove from heat and add liver, eggs, anchovies, and pepper. Mix well and pour into baking pan. Place in another pan with hot water at least half way up the side of the smaller pan, and bake in 325° oven about 1½ hours or until knife comes out clean. Cool before serving. *Makes about 1 quart.*

VARIATIONS: If you like something different every time, try the following variations: (1) use chicken or calves' liver in place of pork; (2) make without white sauce; (3) use cream instead of milk; (4) add 1 teaspoon ground ginger; (5) use salt instead of anchovies; (6) line pan with strips of bacon; (7) line pan with meat aspic.

Mustard Eggs

(Skidne Aeg or Aeg med Sennepsauce)

According to Peter, this dish is traditional on the day before Easter in Denmark.

6 *eggs*
3 *tablespoons butter*
2 *tablespoons flour*
1 *teaspoon dry mustard*

½ *teaspoon curry powder*
1 *cup seasoned beef stock*
1 *tablespoon prepared mustard, or more to taste*

Cook eggs in boiling water for 7 minutes, put in cold water for 1 minute, peel, and keep warm. Melt 2 tablespoons of the butter, add flour, dry mustard, and curry powder, and stir over medium heat for 2 or 3 minutes. Do not let burn. Beat in the stock and cook until thick and smooth. Simmer covered for 5 minutes. Add prepared mustard and remaining 1 tablespoon butter just before serving. Pour over eggs. *Makes 3 or 6 servings.*

Fish Mousse

(Fiskefars)

Many Europeans think that American cooking all comes out of cans and packages labeled TV dinners, but Europe now has lots of packaged, frozen, and processed foods too. And there are some they have always had, such as the *Fiskefars* that one can buy by the pound in Copenhagen fish markets. I often wish I could buy this convenient preparation in America. It can be put to so many uses—formed into dumplings to serve in combination with other fish or shellfish, shaped into balls and served in soup, stuffed in salmon for an elegant party dish. As I have to make my own, I like to turn it into something a bit fancy like this molded mousse.

*3 tablespoons fine bread
  crumbs
2 eggs
Salt
White pepper
1/4 cup milk*

*1 pound fresh fillets of
  pike, haddock, or salmon
3/4 cup heavy cream
1/4 pound butter
3 tablespoons lemon juice*

Bring all ingredients to room temperature. Butter a 1-quart ring mold, sprinkle with breadcrumbs, and shake out excess. Beat eggs with salt and pepper to taste, add milk. Remove any bits of bone and skin from fish, chop, and blend in electric blender together with egg mixture. Empty into mixing bowl and beat in cream slowly with wooden spoon. The mixture should be smooth but not liquid. Drop a teaspoonful of it into boiling water and cook briefly; if it seems too liquid, thicken with a little flour. Or if too firm, thin with milk. Pour into ringmold, cover with aluminum foil, and place in pan with hot water 1" deep. Bake in 300° oven for 1 to 1½ hours, or until knife comes out clean, adding more water to large pan if necessary. Or steam rather than bake if you have a steamer large enough to hold the mold. Melt butter, combine with lemon juice and serve as sauce with mousse, or make a hollandaise sauce or a lobster sauce (Sauce Cardinale). *Makes 4 to 6 servings.*

Poached Codfish with Horseradish Sauce
(*Kogt Torsk med Peberrodsauce*)

1 whole 2- to 3-pound cod, cleaned and head removed
1 small onion
½ cup butter
2 tablespoons grated fresh horseradish
1 bunch parsley
1 cup sliced pickled beets
2 tablespoons capers
1 lemon, cut in wedges

Sprinkle fish with salt, or place it in well-salted water, and let stand for 15 minutes. Rinse with cold water and dry. (If cod has come straight off the fishing boat rather than from the market, you can omit this operation.) Fill a fish-boiler or large kettle with enough cold water almost to cover fish, add onion and 1 tablespoon salt for each 2 quarts water, and lower in fish carefully. Bring water to boil over medium-high heat, uncovered. Skim. Cover and simmer until fish tests done, about 15 minutes. Do not overcook. To make a sauce, melt butter and stir in horseradish. If fresh horseradish is not available, you can make another good sauce by stirring chopped hardboiled egg and a little mustard into the butter. Place fish on serving platter lined with a large napkin; surround it with parsley, beets, capers, and lemon wedges, and serve sauce separately. *Makes 6 servings.*

NOTE: Any leftover poached codfish makes a good salad dressed with sour cream. If you prefer to cook steaks instead of a whole fish, start them in water that is already boiling, skim, and simmer for about 5 minutes. Always serve poached fish on a napkin, to absorb excess moisture. The same goes for asparagus.

Fried Eels
(Stegt Aal)

2 eels, skinned and cut in
  3-inch pieces
½ cup flour
1 teaspoon salt
½ teaspoon pepper

4 tablespoons butter
4 tablespoons lemon juice
4 tablespoons minced par-
  sley
1 lemon, cut in wedges

Eels come to market in various sizes, and one will usually serve two or three people, sometimes four. Ask your fish merchant to skin the eels and cut them in 3-inch pieces. When you get them home, sprinkle generously with salt, let stand for ½ hour, rinse, and dry. Shake the pieces of eel in a bag with the flour, salt, and pepper. Fry gently in butter, turning to brown on all sides, about 20 minutes altogether. Or bake for ½ hour in a hot oven, turning once. Remove to hot plate, add lemon juice to pan, and scrape. More butter may be added and cooked until brown, if desired. A few capers may also be added to the lemon-butter. Pour over eels and garnish with parsley and lemon wedges. Boiled potatoes and creamed spinach are good accompaniments. *Makes 4 to 6 servings.*

Polar Bear's Eye

In Denmark we usually call this dish the Eye of the Sun, but the Arctic name for it is certainly more picturesque. I don't know why polar bears have red eyes, but they do. The dish can be made in individual servings (one egg yolk per person), or two "eyes" on a platter, or a large single "eye" to be mixed at the table and served on small plates. You can dress and arrange the ingredients in separate circles for display, but they taste the same when mixed up. This makes a good first course at dinner, a luncheon dish, or a midnight snack (when it's the Eye of the Midnight Sun). It's also sometimes called a Bird's Nest.

4 large potatoes, boiled, peeled, and diced
2 large beets, boiled, peeled, and diced
1 large sweet onion (raw), peeled and diced

2 2-ounce cans flat fillets of anchovies, chopped
Salt and pepper
4 raw egg yolks

Combine potatoes, beets, onion, and anchovies, retaining the olive oil from the anchovy cans. Add an additional few drops of olive oil if you like, but the mixture should be rather dry. Salt and pepper to taste. Spread evenly on 4 small plates, make a depression in the middle of each, and slip an egg yolk into each depression. At the table each person breaks the egg yolk and mixes it lightly with the other ingredients. The potatoes and beets may be eaten either chilled or lukewarm; I like them better the first way. *Makes 4 generous servings.*

Jansson's Temptation
(Janssons Frestelse)

This popular Swedish casserole makes a nice lunch dish, followed by green salad and cheese.

4 tablespoons butter
2 onions, or leeks, sliced thin
1 pound raw potatoes, peeled and cut in julienne strips
1 2-ounce can flat fillets of anchovies
1 cup heavy cream

Sauté onions in 2 tablespoons of butter until transparent. Butter a shallow baking dish and spread half the potatoes on the bottom of it. Cover potatoes with onions. Then place the anchovies on top of the onions in neat parallel rows. Put the rest of the potatoes on top, and dot with the remaining butter. Bake at 375° for 10 minutes, add half the cream and bake another 10 minutes, then add the rest of the cream and bake about ½ hour or until potatoes test done. *Makes 4 servings, or 6 as a first course.*

Roast Goose Stuffed with Apples and Prunes
(*Gaasesteg*)

This is a traditional dish in Denmark on Christmas Eve, or on any day in the winter, or any time you have a goose. The younger the goose, the tenderer; 8 pounds is fine, and 10 is maximum for roasting.

> 1 *8-pound goose, excess fat removed, well salted and rubbed with lemon inside and out*
> 2 *cups green apples, sliced*
> 2 *cups prunes, soaked, pitted and halved*
> 2 *cups stock*
> 4 *tablespoons red currant jelly*
> 3 *red apples (optional)*

Stuff goose with sliced apples and prunes, truss, and place on its side on the rack of a roasting pan with 1 cup hot stock in the bottom of the pan. Prick gently with fork and roast uncovered at 400° for 1 hour. Prick again and baste every 15 minutes after the first ½ hour. Turn on other side and roast 1 hour more, skimming or pouring off fat and adding stock or water to pan if juices get too brown. Now reduce heat to 325° and roast breast up, still basting and pouring off fat, until goose tests done. The leg joints must move freely—probably another hour or more. Remove goose to serving platter. Pour off remaining fat but leave juices in pan. Add any remaining stock, bring to boil, and scrape pan. Add red currant jelly and stir until well mixed. Or stuff half apples with jelly and use to garnish goose. *Makes 6 servings.*

Pickled Duck
(Spraengt And)

1 4- to 5-pound duck	6 peppercorns
½ lemon	1 onion, sliced
1 cup salt	1 carrot
½ cup sugar	Sprigs of parsley
½ teaspoon saltpeter	1 bay leaf

Remove skin and fat from duck. Assuming you start with a frozen duck, as most people do, this is easiest to accomplish while the duck isn't quite completely thawed out. The more you can remove before cooking the better. You can use duckfat for some kinds of cooking (it does wonders for boiled turnips), and the skin is delicious roasted or broiled, but if most of your friends are dieting the way mine are, you may want to pass these treasures on to a Chinese acquaintance. In any case, they aren't needed for this dish.

When duck is completely thawed, rub it inside and out with the half lemon. Mix together ½ cup salt, ¼ cup sugar, and the saltpeter, (obtainable at drugstores), and rub duck with mixture inside and out. Place in covered bowl in refrigerator for 5 or 6 hours. Dissolve remaining salt and sugar in 4 cups water, bring to boil, and let cool. Pour over duck in bowl, adding more water if necessary to cover duck. Press down with plate so that duck remains immersed in liquid, and refrigerate another 8 to 10 hours.

Rinse and drain duck, discarding brine. Place in pot with water nearly to cover and bring to boil. Skim; add all remaining ingredients, bring to boil, and skim again. Simmer until tender, about 1 hour and 20 minutes. Serve either hot or cold. *Makes 5 servings*.

I usually make a stock of the giblets, adding it to the cooking liquid after the duck is removed, and sometimes I return the carcass to this broth after cutting away the meat. It can then be used to make a sauce or an aspic.

Roast Pheasant with Grapes

If you want tasty and tender roast pheasant you should give some attention to three matters: the birds must be hung for several days, they should be barded or at least the breasts should be covered with fat bacon while roasting, and they should be filled with a stuffing that will add moisture to the meat. If you buy from a butcher instead of hunting your own pheasants, he can take care of the first two requirements. Or when pheasants are unavailable, substitute Cornish game hens and forget about these problems. (But then of course you won't have the taste of pheasant.)

2 pheasants, barded (or 2 1½-pound Cornish game hens)
2 teaspoons salt
½ teaspoon pepper
½ cup dry white wine
2 cups grapes, halved (and seeded if necessary)
2 tablespoons melted butter
½ cup chicken bouillon
2 tablespoons Madeira

Salt and pepper the birds inside and out. Sprinkle cavities with wine and stuff with as many of the grapes as they will hold. Sew up. Place in a casserole or roasting pan with butter, breast side down, and roast uncovered at 450° for 10 minutes. Then turn breast up and roast at same temperature 20 minutes more. Add remaining wine and bouillon to casserole, reduce heat to 350°, and roast ½ hour more, still uncovered, basting every 5 minutes. Remove barding for the final 15 minutes of roasting. Remove birds to platter, add remaining grapes and Madeira to casserole, and cook over high heat until liquid is reduced. *Makes 4 servings (or 2 for hungry hunters).*

Danish Chicken Fricassee

1 3- to 4-pound chicken, whole or cut up	Pinch of thyme
½ lemon	2 cups chicken stock
2 onions, sliced	2 tablespoons butter
2 carrots, sliced	2 tablespoons flour
3 stalks celery, cut in pieces	2 egg yolks, lightly beaten
3 sprigs parsley	4 tablespoons heavy cream
6 peppercorns	3 tablespoons grated fresh horseradish, or to taste
1 bay leaf	Salt and pepper

Rub chicken all over with lemon and place in pot with vegetables, seasonings, and stock. Add water, if necessary, to cover. Bring to boil, cover, and simmer until tender, 35 minutes or more according to size of chicken pieces. Remove chicken. Discard bay leaf, reduce stock to about 2 cups, skim off fat, and strain. Combine butter and flour, and stir in stock to make a sauce. Add egg yolks, cream, horseradish, and salt and pepper to taste. If you cannot get fresh horseradish, flavor the sauce with a little curry powder, lemon juice, or capers. Skin and bone chicken, add to sauce, and heat through, being careful not to boil. (Boiling harms the taste of the horseradish, and it may curdle the sauce.) Serve with rice or boiled new potatoes. Either green or white asparagus is also good with this dish. *Makes 4 to 6 servings.*

Lamb in Dill

This spring-and-summer dish is very popular in Sweden, served with new potatoes and cucumber salad.

5 pounds lamb shoulder or breast, or more if there is lots of bone
1 tablespoon salt
½ cup fresh dill, chopped
2 carrots, chopped fine
2 stalks celery, chopped fine

2 medium onions, chopped fine
12 peppercorns
3 tablespoons butter
3 tablespoons flour
1 tablespoon sugar
¼ cup vinegar
2 egg yolks
½ cup heavy cream

Cut meat in serving pieces, removing most of the fat. Place in pot with salt and water to cover, bring to boil, and skim. Add 1 tablespoon of the dill, together with carrots, celery, onions, and peppercorns, and bring to boil. Skim again. Simmer until thoroughly tender, about 1 hour. Drain broth, skim off fat if possible, and cook over high heat until reduced to about 2 cups. In a large skillet melt 2 tablespoons of the butter, stir in flour with wire whisk, and add broth, stirring rapidly. Cook for about 10 minutes after mixture is smooth. Stir in remaining dill, sugar and vinegar. Blend yolks with cream and stir into mixture off fire. Add meat and reheat to boiling. Add 1 tablespoon butter. *Makes 8 servings.*

Sailors' Stew
(Skipperlabskovs)

One of Peter's favorite Danish dishes, this stew has a great many variations. You can make it equally well with beef, veal, or pork. Sometimes it is made with leftovers. The ingredients can be either cubed or sliced. It can be made on top of the stove or baked in the oven. The liquid used may be either beef stock or beer, or some of each. Peter always used stock, but I think beer is better.

3 tablespoons butter
3 onions, sliced
1½ pounds round steak cut in ½" cubes
Salt
6 peppercorns

6 medium potatoes, peeled and sliced thin
2 cups beer or stock, or half and half
Parsley, chopped

Cook onions in butter until transparent. Remove with slotted spoon to casserole. Brown meat in onion pan, salting to taste. Add to onions in casserole, together with peppercorns and potatoes. Deglaze onion pan with beer and add to casserole. Cover and simmer until tender, about 1½ hours. Or bake for the same length of time in a medium oven. If more liquid is needed, add stock. Sprinkle with chopped parsley. *Makes 4 servings.*

Swedish Hamburger
(Bøf à la Lindstrøm)

A popular classic, this deserves a high place on anybody's list of best ways to cook hamburger. The texture should be very fine, so have the meat ground twice, or grind it yourself, together with the cooked potatoes. Combine the ingredients just before cooking; otherwise the patties may become dry and fall apart.

1 *pound lean beef (sirloin or round), ground twice*
2 *medium boiled potatoes, chopped*
2 *teaspoons salt*
1 *teaspoon pepper*
½ *cup heavy cream*
2 *egg yolks*
2 *tablespoons onion, chopped very fine*
2 *tablespoons pickled beets, chopped*
1 *tablespoon capers, chopped*
2 *tablespoons beet juice*
2 *tablespoons soda water*
2 *tablespoons butter*

Mix meat, potatoes, salt, and pepper together well. Stir in cream and beaten egg yolks. Add remaining ingredients and correct seasoning if necessary. Form into small patties at least 1″ thick and brown quickly in butter, turning only once. The patties should be rare inside. For a variation, make larger patties and cover each with a fried egg. Or for wonderful hot canapés, spread the mixture thickly on small rounds of bread and sauté in butter, first meat side down, then bread side down. *Makes 6 to 8 servings.*

Beef Stroganoff

This has become such a popular international dish that I even had it on a recent visit to Russia, where it's still almost unknown. Some cooks make it with mushrooms, some use more butter and a lot more sour cream than I do, and one recipe I have adds garlic, red wine, and tomatoes. In every case the idea is to use very tender meat and cook it very quickly. Because of the quick cooking it's a nice dish to do at the table, in a chafing dish. Serve it with rice, noodles, or mashed potatoes.

2 pounds beef tenderloin, cut with the grain into thin strips or shoestrings
1 teaspoon salt
1/4 teaspoon pepper
4 tablespoons butter

1 tablespoon flour
1 cup meat stock
1 tablespoon minced shal-lot
1/2 cup sour cream

Salt and pepper the meat and put it aside for 1/2 hour. Melt 2 tablespoons of the butter in a skillet, stir in the flour, add the stock gradually, and cook until somewhat thickened. Now sauté the meat quickly in another pan (or in your chafing dish) in the remaining 2 tablespoons butter and minced shallot, stirring it over high heat for only a minute or two, as in Chinese cooking. Stir the sour cream into the sauce, pour it over the meat, and serve immediately. In this and other dishes requiring sour cream, I often reduce the calories by using half sour cream and half yogurt. *Makes 6 servings.*

Danish Red Cabbage

(Rødkaal)

There's never a Danish Christmas goose without red cabbage and sugar-browned potatoes.

3 *tablespoons butter or goose fat*	¼ *cup water*
1 *tablespoon sugar*	1 *teaspoon caraway seeds*
1 *2-pound red cabbage, finely shredded*	1 *teaspoon salt*
¼ *cup wine vinegar*	1 *teaspoon pepper*
	½ *cup red currant jelly*

Melt sugar and butter in casserole, add cabbage, stir, and cook for a few minutes until well mixed. Add vinegar, water, caraway seeds, salt, and pepper. Cover and cook on low heat for 2 hours. Add a little water during cooking if necessary to prevent burning. If you have leftover vinegar from pickled beets you can use ½ cup of it in place of vinegar and water in this recipe. Add redcurrant jelly, mix well, and taste. Now you can add a little more sugar or vinegar to adjust the sweet-and-sour taste to your preference. This dish may be stored and reheated; in fact, there are people who say it is better that way. *Makes 6 or more servings, depending on appetite.*

Creamed Kale

As a rule I like fresh vegetables better than frozen, and this holds true even for greens such as spinach and kale. But when you make *creamed* kale you may find that you çan hardly tell the difference.

2 packages frozen chopped
kale, or 2 pounds fresh
kale
3 tablespoons butter
3 tablespoons flour

1½ cups milk, stock, or
vegetable water
Salt and pepper to taste
Pinch of cayenne pepper
Pince of mace

Cook frozen kale according to directions on package but reduce cooking time by ⅓. Or cook fresh kale, after removing the toughest parts of the stalks, in minimum water for 20 minutes, then chop. Make a white sauce with all the rest of the ingredients, add kale, and heat through. If the cooked kale has much liquid it should be drained off and put in soup or saved for another use. *Makes 4 to 6 servings.*

Buttermilk Dessert

(Kaernemaelkskoldskal)

In Danish this is called cold buttermilk soup, but I changed the name in English because most people will want to eat it as a dessert. It's always accompanied by oatmeal cookies or small zwieback. I think it's the best thing after a swim, refreshing and reviving, and it makes a good substitute for an ice cream soda. Even people who don't like buttermilk like this.

2 egg yolks
4 tablespoons sugar
Grated rind and juice of 1
lemon

1 teaspoon vanilla extract
1 quart buttermilk
Whipped cream, sweet-
ened (optional)

Beat egg yolks and sugar until pale, using either a wire whisk or electric beater. Beat lemon rind and juice and vanilla into buttermilk, then beat this gradually into the egg mixture. Chill for at least 1 hour. If desired, top with whipped cream just before serving. *Makes 4 to 6 servings.*

Rødgrød Made with Frozen Berries

Rødgrød, the most popular Danish pudding, requires fresh red raspberries and currants, but what can you do when these aren't in season? Use fruit juice that you have put aside for a rainy day, but if you forgot to do that, try the following recipe* from Nika Standen Hazelton's excellent book, *The Art of Danish Cooking*.

> 2 10-ounce packages frozen raspberries, thawed
> 2 10-ounce packages frozen strawberries, thawed
> ⅓ cup cornstarch
> ½ cup water
> 1 tablespoon lemon juice
> Sugar
> ⅓ cup blanched almonds, slivered
> Heavy cream

Combine berries in saucepan. Bring to a boil, stirring occasionally. Strain through fine sieve or purée in blender. Mix cornstarch with ½ cup water to a smooth paste. Bring fruit back to boiling point. Stir cornstarch into fruit. Bring to a boil and cook 3 minutes, stirring constantly. Remove from heat and blend in lemon juice. Pour into glass serving dish and sprinkle top with a little sugar. Chill. Decorate with slivered almonds before serving. Serve with heavy unwhipped cream. *Makes 6 servings.*

*Reprinted by permission of Collins-Knowlton-Wing, Inc. Copyright © 1964 by Nika Standen Hazelton. Published by Doubleday & Company, Inc.

Almond Rice
(Ris à l'Amande)

This dessert is very popular in Denmark. I have tried making it with skimmed milk and a low-calorie topping in place of the whipped cream, and it still tastes good.

> *2 cups milk*
> *½ cup rice, washed*
> *2 tablespoons sugar*
> *4 tablespoons blanched and chopped almonds (not grated)*
> *½ teaspoon vanilla*
> *1 cup heavy cream*
> *1 tablespoon unflavored gelatin (optional)*

Scald milk, stir in rice, and cook over low heat (or in double boiler) until tender—about 30 minutes, depending on type of rice. Do not overcook. Let cool, and mix in sugar, almonds, and vanilla. Chill well. Whip cream until stiff, and fold it in well. If you want to mold the dessert, dissolve the gelatin in 2 tablespoons water and stir it in just before adding the cream. This is the basic dessert. Whether molded or spooned into bowls, it is often decorated with black cherries, fresh orange sections, or crystallized fruits, and served with a thin fruit sauce. It is also served on Christmas Eve, like the dish that follows, with a whole hidden almond. *Makes 4 to 6 servings.*

Rice Pudding with a Hidden Almond
(Risengrød)

Another traditional Danish Christmas dish, this is really more of a porridge than a pudding. Unlike other rice puddings, it has no eggs to thicken and enrich it, but it does have other treasures.

1 cup rice	4 tablespoons butter
4 cups milk	Sugar
½ teaspoon salt	Ground cinnamon
1 large almond, blanched	

Wash the rice well two or three times to remove some of the starch. Bring milk to a simmer, stir in rice, cover, and cook over low heat until rice is tender. Stir to avoid scorching, or cook in a double boiler. Add salt and the single whole almond, and serve while still hot. (Whoever gets the almond in his bowl gets a prize.) Sprinkle each bowl of rice pudding with sugar and cinnamon, add a pat of butter and dribble on some syrup if you like. Raspberry or strawberry syrup (or the juice from these frozen fruits) makes a colorful dish. For an American touch you can try maple syrup, root beer, or Coca-Cola. This may sound very strange, but it's remarkably good, and just the sort of thing the modern Danes enjoy. *Makes 4 servings.*

Apple and Orange Scallop

During the winter, when fresh berries and so many other fruits are not always available, this healthy, refreshing fruit dessert is most welcome. It is from my mother's kitchen, and couldn't be simpler (no cooking required).

4 oranges	½ cup sugar, or more to
3 apples	taste
4 tablespoons lemon juice	

Peel oranges and slice them crosswise, thin. Peel and core apples and slice thin lengthwise. Sprinkle apple slices quickly with lemon juice to prevent darkening. Reserve 3 or 4 of the evenest and best-looking orange slices, and place the rest, together with apple slices, in alternating layers in a glass serving dish, sprinkling each layer lightly with sugar. Place reserved orange slices on top, sprinkle with sugar and remaining lemon juice, and chill for at least 1 hour. *Makes 6 servings.*

Rhubarb and Banana Pie

I like the taste contrast of rhubarb and bananas. Also, this makes an especially good pie to eat à la mode.

2 cups flour	5 stalks rhubarb, chopped
2/3 cup vegetable shortening	2 bananas, sliced
1 egg yolk	1 cup sugar, or more to taste
1 tablespoon milk mixed with 2 tablespoons cold water	1 egg white

Mix flour, shortening, egg yolk, milk and water to make a ball of dough. Wrap it in wax paper and chill in refrigerator 1 hour. Roll out ⅔ of it and line a deep 8″ pie pan with it. Fill with rhubarb, bananas, and lots of sugar. Only after making one or two pies will you know how much sugar suits your taste, but it will probably be more than a cup. Roll out remaining dough, cut in strips, and make lattice top crust for pie. Brush with egg white and bake in 400° oven for ½ hour or until done. Sprinkle with sugar. *Makes 6 servings.*

Macaroon Apricot Tart
(Aprikos Dessert)

This recipe is from the repertoire of my mother's cook. It is very easy and very good. I have sometimes made it with other fruit instead of apricots, such as fresh rhubarb or strawberries, but the tartness of the apricots is especially good in this combination. Incidentally Peter didn't like dried apricots nearly as well as I do, but he liked all the other dried fruits. He munched them as a kind of candy, and he often cooked prunes or peaches to have as compote. He always added a piece of lemon when stewing dried fruits.

1 11-ounce package of dried apricots	½ cup sherry
¾ pound macaroons	1 cup heavy cream, whipped

Cook apricots in water to cover until quite tender but not mushy, drain and cool. Crush macaroons and spread flat on the bottom of a serving dish or pie plate. Spoon sherry over macaroons and let soak in. Arrange apricots evenly on top, and refrigerate. Decorate with whipped cream just before serving. *Makes 6 to 8 servings.*

Spice Cake
(Asta Kage)

This was my favorite cake as a teen-ager.

¼ pound butter	½ teaspoon clove
1 cup sugar	½ teaspoon baking soda
2 eggs, well beaten	4 tablespoons raisins
2 cups flour	2 tablespoons chopped
½ teaspoon cinnamon	candied orange rind
½ teaspoon cardamom	1 cup buttermilk
1 teaspoon ginger	

Cream butter, adding sugar gradually, then eggs. Sift together flour, all ground spices, and baking soda. Add raisins and orange rind to flour and mix until they are coated. Add flour mixture and buttermilk to egg mixture a little at a time, first one, then the other, alternately. When combined, pour into a greased 9″ x 5″ loaf pan and bake at 300° for 1 hour, or until cake tests done. *Makes 6 servings.*

Lemon Mousse
(Citron Fromage)

This popular Danish desert has many variations. It is often made with orange juice and rind or with pineapple or with rum. But I like it best with lemon because of the refreshing taste.

5 eggs, separated	2 tablespoons unflavored
¾ cup sugar	gelatin
1½ tablespoons grated	½ cup strained lemon juice
lemon rind	1 cup heavy cream

Beat egg yolks and sugar until pale and thick. Stir in the lemon rind. Sprinkle gelatin on 6 tablespoons of water; stir and heat gently until dissolved. Add lemon juice. Beat egg whites until stiff. Stir gelatin and juice mixture carefully into yolks. Whip cream and fold it into yolk mixture together with egg whites. Rinse a glass bowl and leave it wet. Pour in mixture and chill for at least 3 hours. Unmold or serve in bowl. Like Court Dessert, this mousse can be decorated with additional whipped cream and grapes if you like. *Makes 8 to 10 servings.*

Court Dessert
(Hofdessert)

This lovely dessert was my favorite as a small child. I often make it today when I have leftover egg whites, but sometimes I also use meringues from a bakery.

4 egg whites
1 cup superfine granulated
    sugar
Pinch of salt
Pinch of cream of tartar
½ teaspoon vanilla

3 cups heavy cream
½ cup chopped almonds
3 ounces sweet chocolate,
    grated coarsely
1 cup green seedless grapes

Beat egg whites stiff with sugar, salt, cream of tartar, and vanilla. Drop tablespoonfuls of mixture onto baking sheet covered with wax paper. Bake at 200° for 1 hour, then turn off oven and leave meringues in it until ready to use (preferably overnight). Whip the cream and put half of it aside. Now arrange a layer of meringues on a round flat serving dish, add a thin layer of whipped cream, a sprinkle of almonds and chocolate, then another layer of meringues, more whipped cream, almonds, and chocolate, making a pyramid and using up all but 2 tablespoons of the chocolate. Top the pyramid with the reserved half of the whipped cream, decorate with remaining chocolate and grapes. Or make individual pyramids in glass sherbet dishes. *Makes 6 to 8 servings.*

Whipped Cream Cones
(Kraemmerhuse med Flødeskum)

You can't very well serve ice cream cones at a dinner party, but here's an adult cone that everyone likes. I think you could also use the cones, without the whipped cream filling, to hold Greenland frozen eggs, which are otherwise a bit tricky to eat unless you're standing outside in sub-zero temperatures.

4 tablespoons butter, melted	2/3 cup flour
1/2 cup sugar	1 cup heavy cream, whipped
2 eggs	Strawberry jam

Combine butter and sugar, beat in eggs one at a time, then flour. Drop spoonfuls of this batter about 4 inches apart on a well-buttered baking sheet. Smooth out with a spatula into thin ovals, and bake for 6 minutes in 300° oven. Pull baking sheet part way out of oven and remove nearest cookies with spatula, rolling each one quickly into a cone while still hot and flexible. (Use gloves for this if you like.) If dough becomes too hard, push back into oven to soften. As each cone is rolled place it onto the neck of a bottle to hold its shape while cooling. Butter baking sheet again for each batch. Just before serving, fill cones with cream, placing a little jam in the center of each. *Makes 8 servings.*

Greenland Coffee

There are no cows in Greenland and consequently there's no fresh cream. Today there may be plenty of canned milk or cream, but in Peter's time the Greenlanders used beaten egg yolks in their coffee with interesting results. (There are plenty of birds and eggs in the Arctic.) Peter introduced this drink to me, and I decided that it tasted so much like zabaglione that we began serving it as dessert.

4 egg yolks   *6 cups hot coffee*
4 tablespoons sugar

Beat egg yolks and sugar together until they are white and foamy. Divide the mixture equally between 6 coffee cups and pour in hot coffee, stirring. *Makes 6 servings.*

Sweet Pancakes

Both Peter and I liked all kinds of pancakes, and we ate a lot of them. Here is a recipe for one of our favorites, a very thin dessert pancake.

1 cup flour	3 eggs, beaten lightly
1 tablespoon sugar	1 tablespoon cognac
½ teaspoon salt	Butter
2½ cups skim milk, or 2 cups milk plus ½ cup water	

Sift flour, sugar, and salt into bowl. Add milk and eggs, a little of each alternately, mixing well to avoid lumps. You can use an electric blender if you have one. Let batter rest for 2 hours in refrigerator. Beat again, adding cognac and 1 tablespoon of melted butter. Heat a couple of tablespoons of butter in skillet and pour in batter to make a pancake 8" or 9" in diameter. Cook until golden on each side, turning once and shaking pan to keep from sticking. Fold pancake over twice and keep in warming oven. Add butter to skillet and stir batter again before pouring in each pancake. Serve with confectioners' sugar and preserves. *Makes 6 servings.*

SECTION TWO

The Mediterranean Sea

THE MEDITERRANEAN SEA

Introduction

I think nearly every northern European feels drawn
to the Mediterranean for its sunshine, its wine, its
free Latin spirit. How lucky anyone is who can go
to live in Italy or southern France, Spain, or
Greece. A fish fresh out of the sea, good bread, a
handful of olives, a few tomatoes, lemons, buds of garlic, a glass
of young local wine—all these commonest items of nourishment
and pleasure are so plentiful and cheap that even a poor man can
eat like a prince.

I first went to France when I was a student, and I still remember the wonderful food at the *pension* where I stayed in Paris
while going to art school. A dessert as simple as Petit—Suisse
with crushed strawberries seemed to me exotic and marvelous
in those days. In fact I still like it, and I'm glad this delicate
French cream cheese is now available in New York. I stayed at
a *pension* where there were a couple of other Danish girls, and
there was a rule that we all had to speak French at the dinner
table until dessert, when we could switch to Danish. Our dinners
were always very proper and quiet through the soup and main
course, the salad and cheese. Then when the dessert arrived we
suddenly found we had lots to say to each other and the whole
room grew very noisy.

I visited the French Riviera many years later, when I discovered that I especially liked the hills and mountain villages that
rise up so abruptly and breathtakingly from the edge of the sea
in many places. I didn't actually drive up to the villages that

perch like eagles' nests on top of the mountain peaks because negotiating the lower *corniches* was enough of a challenge. I'm a slow and cautious driver—far too slow for most of the other tourists and for all the local residents and truck drivers, who kept honking their horns to get me out of their way. But there wasn't any place for me to get, except out into space. And I wanted to glance around, while all they wanted was to get to the next place. Several hours of this can become wearing.

I've had only one visit to Greece, and I'd love to go back. The people are so beautiful and so friendly—without the formal reserve and suspicion of strangers one sometimes finds elsewhere. Is it the sunshine?

There's still much of Italy I haven't seen, but the places I have, made me feel as much at home as if I'd been born there. I'm sure you can like Italy without especially liking pasta, but a little appreciation of the Italian genius with wheat doesn't hurt. (Did Marco Polo really bring spaghetti back from China? And if so, whatever was Italy like before that?) A plate of feathery fresh fettucine is a dish for the Gods.

Peter admired the very neat way some Italians have of eating spaghetti, wrapping it around the tines of a fork as they turn the fork against the bowl of a spoon until all the longest strings have got raveled up. In fact we both always respected neat and efficient ways of eating anything. We always had honey for breakfast at home, and Peter used to classify our weekend guests in Noank as people who could eat the honey without making a mess of the honey pot, and people who couldn't.

I haven't yet visited the eastern end of the Mediterranean or north Africa, but friends tell me that the towns on these shores of the great inland sea are very Mediterranean in character, at least as much influenced by the history and cultures of the Mediterranean as by the deserts and their cultures that lie back from the sea on these sides. Maybe somebody could do a comparative study of Mediterranean civilizations based on their ways of cooking rice, or roasting fish, or preparing an assortment of appetizers, from the *tapas* of a Spanish bar through *antipasti* and their delicious Greek cousins midway between Europe and the Near East, to Turkish *mezeler* and Arab *meze*, the tidbits that always come with a glass of *arak* and often begin a formal banquet.

The first four recipes that follow give a small sampling of this very large repertory. Then come two soups that are worth making just as described, and a third one that ought to be different every time it's made. Fish soups are a staple of the whole Mediterranean, but nobody sets out to follow a recipe, unless it's a restaurant trying to give tourists what they expect in a "real bouillabaisse." Use whatever you have, what's in the market, what's good, what you like.

Peter and I so much preferred fresh cod to salt that I haven't put in any recipes for the dried fish, good though it can be.

Chickens are everywhere in the area; but lacking good grazing land, the Mediterranean doesn't have much beef, and the leading meats are veal (in Italy) and lamb.

Fruit is so popular for dessert (and relatively plentiful) that other kinds of dessert seem unnecessary, at least at the main meals. Pastries, puddings and such tend to be regarded like candy, as things you might have between meals, perhaps with a cup of coffee or tea.

Only three or four recipes in this section present any shopping problem, and substitutions are suggested in case you don't have access to a Near Eastern and a Spanish grocery.

Caviar Appetizer
(Tarama)

The Greeks use pressed, salted carp roe for this appetizer, but a jar of red caviar may be substituted if you can't find *tarama* in a fancy food shop or Middle Eastern grocery. Mix it in a bowl with a wooden spoon, or use an electric blender.

1 8-ounce jar Greek tarama, or red caviar
4 slices white bread, crusts trimmed off

1 clove garlic, mashed
6 tablespoons lemon juice
1 cup olive oil

Moisten bread with water and squeeze it dry. Mix together all ingredients except oil. Add the oil a little at a time, blending or beating to achieve a smooth purée. You may add a little water if it is too stiff at the end, or if it becomes dry from standing. Serve decorated with chopped parsley or fresh coriander,* or with any salad greens or wedges of raw green pepper. Flat Middle Eastern bread and unsalted crackers or Melba toast make good accompaniments. *Makes 8 to 12 appetizer servings.*

Minted Anchovies

Among the many good appetizers from North Africa and the Near East, this is outstanding, and simple.

1 2-ounce can flat fillets of anchovies
2 tablespoons finely chopped fresh mint leaves
½ teaspoon ground nutmeg

Drain the anchovies of oil and let them get dry. Roll them in the mint, then in the nutmeg (not in the nutmeg first, or they will pick up too much of it). If you can't get fresh mint, use dried mint rubbed between the palms of your hands into a

---

*Buy this from a Mexican grocer as *cilantro* or an Oriental grocer as Chinese parsley.

powder; it will give a nice aroma, though not as much taste. Serve with bread or another bland appetizer to balance the saltiness. *Makes 4 servings.*

Brain Salad

Most of my friends have never eaten brains cooked any way except with browned butter and capers, until I serve them this Near Eastern appetizer.

2 *pounds lamb or calves' brains*
1 *teaspoon salt*
4 *tablespoons lemon juice*

2 *tablespoons finely minced onion*
4 *tablespoons minced fresh coriander* or parsley*
4 *tomatoes*

Remove membrane and veins from the brains and soak them in cold water for ½ hour. Boil them in enough water to cover, together with the salt and 1 tablespoon of the lemon juice, until they are tender, about ½ hour. Drain and cool. Slice thin, dress with the remaining lemon juice, minced onion and coriander, and serve with sliced tomato. *Makes 8 appetizer servings.*

*Cilantro or Chinese parsley.

Stuffed Grape Leaves

Here is a way to get some additional use from the bones in a leg
of lamb, which you may have bought to roast or cut up for
shish kebab.

1 12-ounce jar grape leaves	2 cloves garlic, sliced
3/4 pound ground lamb	2 tomatoes sliced
1 cup uncooked rice	2 1/2 cups stock or water
1/2 teaspoon ground cinna-	Salt and pepper
mon	1 lemon, cut in wedges
Lamb bones	

Rinse grape leaves in warm water. Combine lamb (which
you can grind yourself from trimmings, if you bought a leg),
uncooked rice, and cinnamon. Put 1 teaspoon of mixture in center
of each leaf, and roll up from the bottom, folding in the sides,
and ending with the top point. (Remove stems if the leaves have
them.) Don't roll too tightly, for the rice will swell. Put bones
on bottom of large casserole, cover with garlic and tomatoes,
place rolled-up leaves on top, in 2 or 3 layers if necessary, and
add stock with salt and pepper to taste. Cover and cook for 1
hour, or until rice tests done. Serve hot or cold with a wedge of
lemon. *Makes 8 appetizer servings.*

Garlic Soup

I have a Spanish cookbook which says you can make soup from
2 cloves of garlic, a little oil, 1 slice of bread per person, and
enough water for the number of persons to be served—that's all.
This gives me a strong feeling for the poverty of Spain, but
maybe I'm out of date. Anyway, garlic soup is usually made
somewhat richer, as in this version.

6 cloves garlic
6 tablespoons olive oil
Dash of red pepper
6 slices white bread, cubed
6 cups water or stock
Use one or all of the following as garniture:

2 small roast peppers,
  diced
½ pound chorizo (Span-
  ish garlic sausage),
  diced
4 eggs, beaten

Fry garlic in oil with red pepper very briefly, until pale brown; remove and crush. Fry cubes of bread in oil. Do not remove, but add water or stock and crushed garlic. Cover and simmer for ½ hour. Taste and correct seasoning. Then add garniture and simmer 5 minutes longer. If you use eggs, stir soup while it simmers. *Makes 6 servings.*

Gazpacho

Craig Claiborne calls gazpacho "a liquid salad from Spain." Of the many variations, I think this recipe is one of the best.

2 slices white bread, crusts
  removed
2 large tomatoes, peeled,
  seeded, and diced
1 clove garlic, crushed
2 tablespoons olive oil
2 tablespoons vinegar
1 small onion, minced
1 pimiento, diced

1 teaspoon salt
½ cup diced hardboiled
  egg
½ cup diced green pepper
½ cup diced seeded
  cucumber
½ cup croutons browned
  in olive oil seasoned with
  garlic

Crumble or tear bread into small bits, and place in blender with next 7 ingredients. Add enough cold water to make a fairly thick soup, and blend until smooth. Chill in refrigerator for 1 hour. Serve garnished with a little of each of the four remaining ingredients, or let your guests do their own garnishing. The vegetables for garnishing may be dressed in more oil and vinegar. *Makes 4 servings.*

Venetian Fish Soup

4 *pounds whole fresh fish,*
such as bass or mackerel
4 *cups water*
2 *bay leaves*
1 *onion stuck with 2*
cloves
3 *sprigs parsley*
2 *teaspoons salt*

6 *peppercorns*
2 *teaspoons ground ginger*
½ *cup olive oil*
2 *cloves garlic*
½ *teaspoon oregano*
1 *cup dry white wine*
1 *cup canned Italian*
peeled tomatoes

Buy 2 or 3 small fish of different kinds, have them cleaned and scaled, but heads and tails left on. Wash them well when you get them home, and cut into small pieces (with or without bone depending on size of fish—the pieces should be bite-sized, not diced). Make a stock by simmering the fish heads and tails and any other trimmings in water with bay leaves, onion, parsley, salt, and peppercorns, for 1 hour. Strain and discard solids. Dust fish lightly with ginger and fry in olive oil, seasoned with garlic and oregano, until lightly browned. Do not remove fish from oil, but add stock, wine, and tomatoes, and simmer covered for 10 minutes. *Makes 4 servings as a main dish.*

Swordfish on Skewers

If restaurant menus are any indication, swordfish is a favorite American dish. Yet swordfish steaks are so often dry and un-interesting. Here is a Turkish way of preparing this exceptional fish that brings out its best qualities.

2 pounds swordfish cut in large cubes
½ cup olive oil
½ cup lemon juice
12 bay leaves

1 lemon cut in thin semi-circles
¼ cup chopped parsley
Salt and pepper to taste

Marinate the fish in half the oil and half the lemon juice, with bay leaves, for 2 hours. Place fish on skewers, alternating with bay leaves and lemon slices. Grill over hot charcoal for 10 minutes, turning frequently and basting with any remaining marinade. Serve with sauce made of the rest of the oil, lemon juice, parsley, salt and pepper. Vegetables such as mushrooms, peppers, and tomatoes may be cooked on separate skewers (after similar marinating), either at lower heat or for a shorter time. *Makes 4 servings.*

Codfish Florentine

Peter and I have both eaten a lot of fresh cod, a fish so common that some people disdain it. I don't think the simple but elegant dish that follows is any better when made with sole, or chicken, or (most popular of all) poached eggs.

1½ *pounds cod fillets*	*Dash of mace or fenu-*
1½ *pounds fresh spinach*	*greek**
3 *tablespoons butter*	4 *tablespoons grated Par-*
3 *tablespoons flour*	*mesan cheese*
½ *teaspoon salt*	4 *lemon wedges*
1½ *cups milk*	

Simmer the fish in salted water until it tests done with fork. Drain. Cook spinach until barely done. Drain and chop. Make a white sauce from all the remaining ingredients except the cheese and lemon. Mace is traditional for seasoning spinach, but fenu-greek makes an interesting variation. Place spinach in bottom of baking dish, cod fillets on top of spinach, and cover with white sauce. Sprinkle with cheese and brown under broiler. Serve with lemon wedges. *Makes 4 servings.*

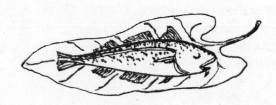

* Ground fenugreek, an essential ingredient of all curry powders, is avail-able on the spice shelves of most supermarkets and fancy food stores. Too much of it can be rank, so sprinkle with care.

Mussels Marinière

When you get the mussels home from the market or the seashore, it's worth a little extra attention to make this dish come out as a simple delight instead of a gritty soup. Throw away any mussels that are broken, or open, or whose shells move under light pressure (they may be full of sand). Keep the good ones in cold water. Scrape off the beard, scrape and scrub the shells, and change the water several times, until no more sand appears.

3 quarts mussels
2 sprigs parsley
2 small onions
1 small carrot, sliced
1 bay leaf
Pinch of thyme

1 cup white wine
4 tablespoons butter
2 tablespoons chopped
parsley
½ clove garlic, minced

Put the mussels in a large casserole with sprigs of parsley, onions, carrot, bay leaf, thyme, and 2 cups of water. Cook just until shells open. Remove mussels from broth and break off the empty half of each shell (throwing away any that refuse to open). Add wine, butter, chopped parsley, and garlic to broth and cook for 3 minutes. Add salt if necessary and pepper if you like it. Return mussels to broth and cook 3 minutes more. Some people like to strain the broth, thicken with eggs and cream, etc., but this begins to get away from the simple sailors' dish that *moules marinières* are supposed to be. *Makes 4 servings.*

Eels in Red Wine
(Lamproie Bordelaise)

Maybe I shouldn't include a recipe for eels because most Americans don't like them. But most Europeans do. And there are many Italian–Americans and French–Americans and Belgian–Americans and Danish–Americans and others who eat them here. And eels are available in many fish markets (as well as, chances are, in your local stream). So here goes—my favorite classic recipe for eels cooked with leeks and red wine, as they do it in Bordeaux. Maybe the leeks will intrigue you enough to make you like the eels. Incidentally, eels are not snakes, they're fish. And they do have scales, but so small you can't see them. In Denmark they say that if a drunkard finds a live eel in his glass it will cure him of the habit. I wouldn't be surprised; it would cure me too.

½ pound salt pork, diced	3 pounds eels, cleaned and
1 large carrot, sliced thin	skinned, cut in 3" pieces
1 medium onion, sliced thin	2 cups red wine, preferably Bordeaux
1 clove garlic	8 small leeks, white part only, well washed
1 bay leaf	5 tablespoons butter
4 sprigs parsley	3 tablespoons flour
1 stalk celery, with leaves, cut up	Salt and pepper
Pinch of thyme	

Fry salt pork in casserole until lightly browned. Remove but leave fat. Cover bottom of casserole with carrots and onions, adding garlic, bay leaf, parsley, celery, and thyme. Place eels on top, and cover with red wine. Cover casserole, bring to boil, and cook on low heat for 15 minutes. In another pan, brown the leeks in 2 tablespoons butter. Then add the salt pork and pieces of eel from casserole. Work together remaining butter and flour, and add a little at a time to casserole, continuing to cook sauce. When well-blended, put sauce through a sieve and add to pan with eels. Cover and cook on low heat for 20 minutes. Season with salt and pepper to taste. *Makes 4 servings.*

Spaghetti with Clam Sauce
(*Linguini alla Vongole*)

If you choose to make this white clam sauce with fresh cherry-stones the taste and texture may be slightly better (be sure not to overcook the clams), but it's a bit tricky to mince raw clams and I save trouble by using canned ones.

1 pound linguini	*1 clove minced garlic*
3 tablespoons olive oil	*6 tablespoons minced*
1 tablespoon flour	*parsley*
2 10½-ounce cans minced	*6 tablespoons butter*
clams	

Boil the linguini in well-salted water for 10 minutes, or just until it tests done. Meanwhile, in a sauce pan stir flour into oil, add juice from clams, and garlic. If necessary to make a smooth sauce, add additional bottled clam juice or water. Add minced clams and parsley, and heat through. This should be a fairly thick sauce. Place 1 tablespoon of butter on each dish of linguini and add hot sauce. *Makes 6 servings.*

Paella

It seems to me *paella* was practically unknown in America when
Gjon Mili used to serve it to us at the Christmas parties in his
studio on 23rd Street, where Eliot Elisofon joined in with the
cooking and Alexander Schneider played his violin, and there
were hours of dancing to good phonograph records. Today *paella*
has become popular, and most people cook it in a covered pot.
The Spanish way is to do it uncovered, in a wide flat dish called
a *paella*. This produces very firm rice, sometimes with a bit of
crust. Put in as many different things from the sea as you like,
plus pork in some form, and chicken. I use Cornish game hens
in place of chicken so that the pieces will be smaller and more
managable in the pot. For the same reason I prefer mussel shells
to big heavy clam shells. But if you have a big enough skillet, the
sky's the limit.

2 Cornish game hens, disjointed
Salt
Bay leaf
1 cup olive oil
½ pound chorizo (Spanish garlic sausage), or hot Italian
  sausage
2 cups rice
1 large onion, chopped
1 cup canned Italian peeled tomatoes, drained
4 cups chicken stock
1 pound shrimps, peeled and deveined
2 pounds mussels in shells
½ teaspoon saffron, soaked in 2 tablespoons stock
2 cloves garlic, minced
½ cup minced parsley
1 package frozen peas

Simmer the Cornish game hens until tender in 4 cups water with salt, bay leaf, and any herbs you like in a stock. Drain and cool. Heat ½ cup oil in your widest skillet or casserole, add pieces of game hen and sausage cut in thin slices. Sauté 10 minutes or until hen is brown, turning to prevent sticking. Add rice, stir, and cook on high fire for a few minutes. Then leave on low fire (but don't let rice get very brown) while you combine in a sauce pan the remaining ½ cup oil, onion (cook these two together until onion is translucent), tomatoes, and 4 cups stock from the chicken. Boil together for 5 minutes, then add this a little at a time to the casserole. Turn the fire high again to give the rice a good start with the liquid, then reduce it after 5 minutes to low. Allow to cook on low fire for ½ hour or until rice is barely tender. Do not add more liquid. As soon as rice begins to be done (or 5 minutes before, if you can guess), add the shrimps, the mussels (cleaned and tested for sand traps as described under Mussels Marinière), and the saffron. Stir and keep on low fire until mussel shells open. Then add garlic, parsley, and peas which have been partly thawed. Stir, and allow to cook or stand for 5 minutes more (until peas are ready). *Makes 6 or 8 servings.*

Chicken Breasts in Vermouth

Chicken breasts are nice when you want a light but elegant main course at a dinner with a good deal of other food. Butchers will bone them for you, but it's so easy to do that you might as well do it yourself and have the skin and bones for stock. The main thing to keep in mind is that the longer you cook a chicken breast the drier and tougher it gets (raw chicken is the tenderest of all, see Chicken Sashimi, p. 141), so cook for the bare minimum of time to get rid of the pink juice.

4 half chicken breasts
Salt and white pepper
1 tablespoon oil
2 tablespoons butter
1 tablespoon minced shallots, or white part of scallions

½ cup dry vermouth
2 teaspoons flour
½ cup chicken stock
½ teaspoon tarragon
2 tablespoons heavy cream

Sprinkle chicken breasts with salt and pepper and brown quickly on both sides in oil and butter. Test by pressing with fingers or knife, and remove to hot platter as soon as pink color is gone from inside (about 5 minutes). Add shallots to pan and cook for 2 minutes, then add vermouth, swirl, and scrape pan. (In place of all dry vermouth, I sometimes use half dry, half sweet, for a more pungent taste.) Add flour, chicken stock, and tarragon, and cook for 2 minutes. Add cream, heat through, and pour over chicken. *Makes 4 servings.*

Turkish Roast Chicken

Stuffed with rice, raisins, and nuts—saturated with the taste of fresh lemon—who could ask for a better roast chicken?

1 chicken liver, chopped
1 cup cooked rice
2 tablespoons butter
¼ cup raisins

½ cup pine nuts or crushed
   walnuts
Salt and pepper
1 4-pound roasting chicken
½ cup fresh lemon juice

Combine chopped chicken liver, cooked rice, butter, raisins, nuts, adding salt and pepper to taste. Stuff chicken and skewer or sew up. Rub with lemon juice. Roast covered, breast side down, in a 300° oven for 1 hour and 20 minutes, then uncovered, breast up, at 350° for 1 hour, basting every 20 minutes with remaining lemon juice and accumulating pan juices. *Makes 4 servings.*

Veal Scallops with Ham
(*Saltimbocca*)

This is one of those dishes where the result depends very much on the high quality of the ingredients—and on limiting the cooking time carefully.

2 pounds small veal scal-
   lops, thin and well-
   pounded
½ pound prosciutto

Leaves of fresh or dried sage
3 tablespoons butter
Salt and pepper
½ cup dry white wine

Trim any gristle from the cutlets and pound them to an even thinness. Cut prosciutto slices to cover cutlets, and fasten together with small bamboo skewers or toothpicks, putting a small leaf of fresh sage or a few shreds of dried sage in between. Sauté in the butter for 3 minutes on the ham side, then 5 minutes on the veal side. Remove to hot platter or plate and season to taste. (Remember, the ham may have quite a lot of salt.) Add wine to pan, scrape and swirl around until liquid is reduced, and pour over meat. *Makes 6 servings.*

Veal with Tuna Sauce
(*Vitello Tonnato*)

I keep meeting people who don't know this Italian dish, and I'm always a little surprised because it's said to be a classic. Whether or not it's true, there's a story I like about its invention. At a certain season or a certain monastery in Italy where the monks were allowed to eat nothing but fish, the fathers grew tired of this limited diet one day, threw a young calf into the nearest stream, and pulled it out with a fish net, exclaiming on the beauty of this strange new species of marine life. To complete the ritual, they masked the cooked veal with a fish sauce, and so was born one of the nicest dishes ever conceived for a hot summer's day. It's especially good for a party, as it isn't hard to make, and you do all the work ahead. I usually serve it with either plain cold rice or Green Pilaf (see recipe in Section 7) and a salad of string beans or tomatoes.

5 *pounds rolled boned leg of veal (no fat added)*
2 *7-ounce cans tuna with oil*
½ *cup olive oil*
2 *2-ounce cans flat fillets of anchovies*
2 *medium onions, chopped*
4 *stalks celery, chopped*
2 *cloves garlic, chopped*
5 *sprigs parsley*

2 *pinches thyme*
2 *bay leaves*
1 *teaspoon pepper*
Salt to taste
3 *cups white wine or dry vermouth*
1 *cup mayonnaise, or to taste*
2 *tablespoons lemon juice, or to taste*
5 *tablespoons capers*

Put all ingredients except last three in a heavy casserole. Be cautious with the salt because anchovies have a lot of it. Bring to boil, cover, and simmer until meat is tender, at least 2 hours. Let cool in broth and refrigerate. When ready to serve, remove

meat and slice thin. Strain cold broth or purée it in blender. Stir in mayonnaise and lemon juice to taste. The sauce should have a creamy consistency. Add capers. *Makes about 10 servings.*

Veal Scallops with Cheese

This dish, made with large veal scallops or cutlets, is for people who really like cheese.

6 ½"-thick veal scallops cut from the rib
1 tablespoon olive oil
3½ tablespoons butter
Pepper

6 thin slices of prosciutto or boiled ham
3 tablespoons flour
1½ cups cream
1 cup grated Parmesan cheese

Dry the veal and sauté for 3 minutes in oil and 1 tablespoon of the butter over high heat on one side only. Arrange in shallow baking pan, browned side down, and sprinkle with pepper. Cover each piece of veal with a slice of ham. Combine the rest of the butter, flour, and cream to make a thick white sauce. Beat in the cheese. The sauce should be very thick, like paste. Spread on top of the ham about ½" thick, using a spoon or spatula. Bake uncovered in 450° oven for 10 minutes. *Makes 6 servings.*

93

Braised Veal Knuckle
(*Osso Buco*)

Osso buco comes from the south (Italy) but is well suited to northern climates. It makes a hearty dinner on a cold winter evening. Just remember to get bones with plenty of meat on them, and cook them long enough for the cartilage to soften.

3 *pounds veal knuckle or shank*	1 *clove garlic, minced*
Flour	½ *cup dry white wine or vermouth*
Salt and pepper	1 *tablespoon tomato paste*
2 *tablespoons olive oil*	1 *cup beef stock*
2 *tablespoons butter*	2 *tablespoons chopped parsley*
1 *carrot, sliced*	
1 *stalk celery, sliced*	1 *tablespoon grated lemon peel*
1 *onion, sliced*	

Have butcher saw bones into 2- to 3-inch pieces. Dredge with flour seasoned with salt and pepper. Heat oil and butter together in large casserole and brown veal knuckles on all sides. Add carrot, celery, onion, and garlic, cover, and cook for 5 minutes. Add wine, tomato paste, and stock, and simmer for 1 to 1½ hours. Strain sauce and pour over meat. Sprinkle each serving with parsley and lemon peel. *Makes 4 servings.*

Veal Scallops with Lemon

Small thin scallops of veal are delicious cooked in Marsala, or vermouth, or white wine, but my favorite of all styles is this one with lemon juice.

1½ pounds small veal scal-lops, pounded very thin	*2 tablespoons butter*
½ cup lemon juice	*2 tablespoons olive oil*
Flour	*Salt and pepper*
	¼ cup chopped parsley

Marinate the scallops in the lemon juice for 1 hour at room temperature. Drain well, flour lightly, and sauté in oil and butter until just cooked through, about 3 minutes on each side. Remove to hot platter, add salt and pepper to taste. Add lemon marinade to pan, scrape, and cook for 1 minute. Add parsley, heat through, and pour over scallops. *Makes 4 servings.*

Stuffed Zucchini

A giant zucchini may serve 4 people. A large one will serve 2. One person can eat both halves of a small one, or even 3 or 4 halves of the smallest. So it's hard to say exactly how many to buy, but large ones will hold the stuffing better and look more spectacular on the plate.

2 *large zucchini*	4 *tablespoons pine nuts*
1 *cup lean ground lamb or*	1 *small can (1 cup) tomato*
beef	*sauce*
1 *cup cooked rice*	2 *teaspoons oregano*
2 *tablespoons olive oil*	

Scrub zucchini but do not peel them. Cut them in half lengthwise and scoop out at least half of the pulp. Chop pulp and combine with meat, rice, oil, and nuts. Stuff zucchini halves with mixture and place in ovenproof dish. Spoon 4 tablespoons of tomato sauce over and around each half. (You can of course make your own sauce from fresh tomatoes, but I like the taste of this convenient canned sauce. Just make sure you get the sauce, not the paste, for you need the water that's in it.) Sprinkle with oregano. Bake at 350° for ½ hour or until thickest part of zucchini tests done with fork. *Makes 4 servings.*

Lamb and Eggplant Casserole
(*Moussaka*)

This casserole is most often made with eggplant and ground lamb, but there's no limit on the variations, either in Greece (its country of origin) or in our kitchen. In place of lamb, use beef or pork or chicken. And include tomatoes, mushrooms, carrots, asparagus, zucchini, artichokes, potatoes—whatever you like.

1 *large eggplant, sliced thin*
1/4 *cup vinaigrette sauce*
1 *pound lean ground lamb*
  or beef
2 *tablespoons butter*
2 *tablespoons flour*

1 *cup stock*
1/4 *cup milk*
Salt and pepper to taste
1/2 *cup grated cheese (1/2*
  Swiss, 1/2 Parmesan, or as
  you like)

Coat the eggplant with vinaigrette and bake in hot oven until soft. (This cooks it using less oil than if you sauté it.) Pan-broil meat, breaking it up with a fork. Put 1/2 the slices of eggplant in a baking dish, cover them with the crumbled meat, then add the remaining slices of eggplant. Cover with a white sauce made from butter, flour, stock and milk. Sprinkle cheese on top, and bake at 400° for 1/2 hour. The top should form a brown crust. *Makes 4 servings.*

Lamb Shish Kebab

We sometimes did this dish at our outdoor barbecue in Noank.

2 *pounds lean lamb, cubed*
  and well trimmed
2 *tablespoons olive oil*
2 *tablespoons wine vinegar*

1 *teaspoon dried marjoram*
6 *peppercorns, crushed*
  coarsely
Salt

Marinate lamb for 2 hours in mixture of oil, vinegar, marjoram, and peppercorns. Thread on skewers and broil over hot charcoal or under a high gas flame, basting with any remaining marinade and turning frequently. Cooking time will depend on size of meat cubes and heat of fire, but 15 minutes may be enough. Salt when cooking is done. *Makes 4 servings.*

Chello Kebab

This is the Persian national dish, I believe; at least it's so popular that there are restaurants in Persia serving nothing else. Yet somebody told me the Persians eat more bread than anybody else on earth. How can they eat so much bread and this rice dish too? A mysterious and wonderful people. Anyway, this dish is actually two separate dishes: yogurt-marinated lamb on a skewer (shish kebab) and rice (pilaf).

Persian Shish Kebab

3 *pounds lean cubes of lamb*	1 *onion, grated*
1 *cup (1 carton) yogurt*	*Salt and pepper*
	Powdered sumac

Marinate lamb in yogurt with onion for 1 or 2 days. (Yogurt is an excellent marinade all by itself, because it contains the acid to tenderize the meat fibers and the fat to swell out the connective tissues.) Broil on skewers (preferably over hot charcoal) for about 15 minutes, turning often. Salt and pepper to taste, and if you want to be really Persian, sprinkle with powdered sumac, which you can buy at a Near Eastern grocery. *Makes 4 generous servings.*

Persian Pilaf

2 *cups rice*
6 *tablespoons butter*
½ *teaspoon saffron, soaked in 2 tablespoons warm water*
1 *large onion, sliced thin, or 1 medium potato, sliced thin*

The idea is to form a golden crust on the bottom of the pot, which will be on top of the rice when you turn it out. Some cooks do this with nothing but rice, but it is easier with a little onion or potato. First, half-cook the rice in lots of boiling salted water and drain. Melt 3 tablespoons of the butter in the bottom of a heavy casserole and add the sliced onion or potato sprinkled with the saffron. Pile rice on top in a cone with a small air hole down the center. Sprinkle remaining 3 tablespoons of butter, melted, over rice, and put lid on casserole with 2 or 3 layers of paper towels under it to absorb moisture. Cook on very low fire until rice is done and bottom has formed crust. Set casserole briefly in water to help loosen crust. Spoon rice onto warm platter, scrape or pry up crust from bottom of casserole, and place it on top of rice. *Makes enough for 4 hungry Persians or 6 to 8 ordinary servings.*

Persian Spinach and Parsley Omelet

Less rich than most omelets and soufflés, this dish has an intense green-vegetable freshness.

1 pound fresh spinach	6 eggs
2 cups chopped parsley	Salt and pepper
1 large leek, chopped fine	3 tablespoons butter

Cook spinach (with water that clings to leaves after washing) until barely wilted. Drain, chop fine, and cool. Wilt parsley and leek, then cool. Beat eggs, add salt and pepper to taste, add vegetables. Heat 2 tablespoons of butter in a heavy pan with a cover. Pour in mixture, cover, and cook on low heat until eggs set. Loosen carefully and invert onto warm plate. Add remaining butter to pan, slide in omelet, cover and cook until lightly browned. Cut in wedges like a pie, and serve as a vegetable course at dinner, or as an appetizer with yogurt dressing (yogurt with salt, onion or garlic, or any herbs you like). *Makes 6 servings.*

Roast Eggplant

This is a dish to prepare whenever you have a charcoal fire going for other things, but you can also roast the eggplant in the gas flame of your range (making something of a mess on the range) or under a high broiler. The idea is both to cook the eggplant and char the skin, so that some of the smoky charred flaver will remain in the dish.

2 medium eggplants	2 cloves garlic, mashed or
1 cup yogurt	minced fine
	1 teaspoon salt

Cook whole eggplants until flesh is tender, turning to char skin on all sides. Peel and discard most of skin, but leave any bits that adhere to the flesh. Chop flesh and place in skillet with yogurt, garlic, and salt. Stir and heat through, but do not bring to boil. *Makes 6 servings.*

Ratatouille

A friend of mine developed this way of cooking ratatouille so that all the lovely flavors of the vegetables are retained but the oil-soaked richness of the traditional Provençale dish is reduced.

2 tablespoons olive oil
1 large onion, thinly sliced
4 cloves garlic, minced
1 large eggplant, cut in small cubes
2 fresh tomatoes, peeled and seeded, or 1 cup canned
   Italian peeled tomatoes
2 small zucchinis, sliced thin
Any or all of the following:
   green peppers
   pimientos
   fresh fennel
   hearts of celery
   capers
   parsley
   basil
   oregano
Salt and pepper to taste

All vegetables should be cut small enough to cook quickly. Sauté onion in oil until translucent. Add garlic and any dried herbs you are using, and cook for 1 minute more. Add all vegetables and stir over high heat until they begin to cook. Then turn heat low, cover, and cook only 10 minutes, or until hardest parts of eggplant test done. Salt and pepper to taste, and if you especially like its taste, dribble one more tablespoon olive oil over vegetables. *Makes 6 servings.*

Chard with Chick Peas

This delicious Arab dish serves as an appetizer, a cold vegetable course, or salad.

2 *pounds fresh Swiss chard,* *or 2 packages frozen* *chard*	2 *medium onions, chopped*
	6 *cloves garlic, minced*
1 *can chick peas, drained*	¼ *cup chopped fresh cori-* *ander* leaves
4 *tablespoons olive oil*	6 *tablespoons lemon juice*

Boil fresh chard, stems first until tender, then leaves for 5 minutes, and add chick peas to heat through. Fry onions in oil until brown; add garlic and coriander to heat through. Add this to chard and chick peas, simmer for 5 minutes, add lemon juice, and chill. *Makes 6 servings.*

Salade Nicoise

Served beside the swimming pool of our hotel in Monte Carlo, this seemed to me the perfect lunch. It's certainly the king of all tuna fish salads, but it can be made only when first-quality fresh tomatoes are available. Other ingredients vary, but no celery, cabbage, or lettuce should find their way in.

1 *7-ounce can tuna fish in olive oil*
2 *large tomatoes*
1 *2-ounce can fillets of anchovies, diced*
10 *black olives, pitted and halved, or 20 small French olives* *if you can find them*
1 *hardboiled egg, quartered*
½ *large green pepper, coarsely chopped*
1 *teaspoon capers*

Cilantro or Chinese parsley.

Available fresh herbs such as tarragon, chervil, basil, chopped
   chives
Vinaigrette dressing heavy with garlic and mustard

Choose the finest quality solid tuna and break it into chunks.
Cut the tomatoes into bite-sized chunks, peeling and seeding or
not, as you like. Combine all ingredients. This makes a rather
purist version. Suitable additions include artichoke hearts, green
beans, potatoes, and other cooked vegetables. But be careful not
to deprive the salad of its fresh crisp quality by putting in too
much soft cooked food. *Makes 2 servings.*

Caramel Custard
(Flan)

The traditional way to make this rich Spanish custard is to boil
the milk down to half quantity, but you can save time by using
canned evaporated milk.

1 cup sugar	2 eggs plus 3 additional egg
2 cups undiluted evapora-	yolks, beaten
ted milk	1 teaspoon vanilla
1/4 teaspoon salt	

Melt ½ cup of the sugar in a heavy skillet, stirring constantly. Pour into a warm mold, and turn the mold to coat the
bottom evenly. Scald the milk, add the remaining sugar and salt,
and when the sugar is dissolved, pour slowly into the beaten
eggs, beating constantly. Add vanilla and mix well. Pour into quart
mold, set in pan of hot water, and bake in 325° oven for 1¼
hours or just until firm. Remove from hot water, and chill. Invert on serving dish. I like to use a ring mold, and many Danes
would fill the center with caramel-flavored whipped cream, but
I don't find this extra richness necessary. *Makes 6 servings.*

Sweet Couscous

This is a dessert *couscous*, the delicious rolled-wheat cereal of North Africa and the Near East. If you can't find a package of *couscous* in a gourmet shop or Near Eastern grocery, substitute farina.

1 package (500 grams)* couscous, *or* 1 pound farina	1 tablespoon grated orange rind
1 cup boiling water	2 ounces sweetened chocolate, grated
12 dates, pitted and halved	1 teaspoon cinnamon
½ cup blanched almonds	2 ounces (½ stick) butter
½ cup shelled pistachio nuts	½ cup sugar syrup
½ cup currants	2 tablespoons orange flower or rose water

Pour the boiling water over the *couscous*, stir, and let stand for 10 minutes. Place in cheesecloth inside steamer, over boiling water, and let the steam rise through it for 15 minutes. Stir every 5 minutes, and the last time, place all but a few of the dates on top to get soft and moist. Now combine all remaining ingredients in blender (or in mortar), and when well blended, mix into *couscous* with a fork and fingers. Decorate top of dish with halves of dates. *Makes 6 servings.*

Mocha Mousse

When fish is the main course, I sometimes feel like making a rich dessert, and I find that most people like mousse. If many of your guests are dieting (as mine are), you can use low-calorie

---

*The grain is packed in North Africa or France in packages this size, equal to about 1 pound 2 ounces.

substitutes for the cream and sugar. In place of the cognac or rum you can substitute ½ teaspoon of vanilla for flavoring.

3 eggs, separated	*tersweet chocolate*
½ cup sugar	*1 tablespoon unflavored*
½ cup strong black coffee	*gelatin*
1 tablespoon cognac or rum	*2 cups heavy cream,*
2 tablespoons grated bit-	*whipped*

Beat egg yolks until light. Beat in sugar gradually; mixture will become pale and thick. Add coffee, cognac, and chocolate, stirring in well. Soften gelatin in ¼ cup cold water and heat in double boiler until fully dissolved. Add to mixture and blend well (I use an electric blender). Cool until it starts to thicken at the edges. Beat egg whites until stiff and fold in, together with whipped cream. Pour into serving dish and chill until set. *Makes 8 servings.*

Sicilian Peach Sherbet

2 *cups crushed ripe*   1 *tablespoon lemon juice*
  peaches   1 *egg white*
1 *cup orange juice*   Sugar

If good fresh peaches are not available, you can make this simple dessert with canned or frozen fruit. Combine peaches, orange and lemon juice, and beat until well blended. Beat egg white with 1 tablespoon sugar, add to fruit, and beat together. Add more sugar to taste. Pour into freezing tray and chill in freezer until almost firm. Empty into bowl and beat again until smooth. Return to freezer and stir every hour until serving. *Makes 8 servings.*

SECTION THREE

The Red and Arabian Seas

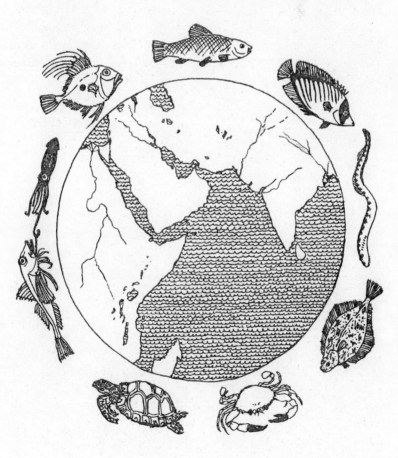

THE RED AND ARABIAN SEAS

Introduction

THE Arabian Sea and Indian Ocean are a focus for the meeting of Arab, East African, and Indian (or Indo–Pakistani–Ceylonese) cooking. Each of these is complicated and different enough to deserve a whole chapter, or even a book. And for India, it might even be four books, one for Punjab and the north, one for Bengal, one for Gujerat, and one for the whole south. India is really more than a single country. in its variety of people, natural resources, climate, and styles of cuisine; it's a whole subcontinent, with about as much land and as many people as all of western Europe.

We had many Indian friends during Peter's years at the United Nations. One of his fellow journalists there, the correspondent of the Madras *Hindu*, even had a son who qualified for the exclusive club of people born on Peter's birthday, February 20th. His affection for Indians still didn't change Peter's aversion to very spicy foods, and I don't have much appetite for curries that set fire to the roof of your mouth. But neither did most of our Indian friends. Perhaps they reduced the hot peppers in the dishes they served to us and the recipes they gave me. In any case my Indian recipes, while far from bland, won't sear your palate or upset your digestion.

The Italians know how to use just a touch of fresh hot green chili peppers in their cooking, and many Indians do likewise. If you don't like even a suspicion of sharpness, then eliminate green chilis, cayenne and black pepper entirely (the following recipes will still be good without them), or substitute sweet green peppers for the hot ones.

Some Indians even dislike the pungency of onions and garlic; and you can leave these out, put both of them in, substitute one for the other—do pretty much as you like with them in these recipes.

The shopping problem for these dishes is not so great as for some other styles of cooking, particularly Japanese. And I feel fairly free about substitutions. Okra is generally available frozen, and there's nothing else quite like it, but various kinds of beans are good in its place. *Bulgur* is sold in health food stores as well as Near Eastern groceries. Chinese grocers carry both ginger root and fresh coriander (Chinese parsley), and fresh ginger turns up in several other markets as well. The coriander will appear in a Mexican market as *cilantro*, if you have one; or you can substitute watercress or parsley if necessary. The basic Indian spices such as turmeric and cumin are now in all supermarkets.

This section contains one of the great fancy rice dishes of the world, the *biryani* of Pakistan and north India. My version is a relatively simple one, but it gives a good idea of the richness of the dish. *Biryani* is usually made in much larger quantity, for parties, and turned out on a tray, where it is piled up in a mound and decorated with additional bits of richness and color such as nuts, butter, grains of colored rice, and thin sheets of edible gold and silver. I cook it in a pretty enameled cast iron casserole and leave it there for serving just for convenience.

In India many strict vegetarians and people who live inland eat no fish. But practically everyone who lives near the long seacoast is a fish-eater, and so are the people in such great river areas as Bengal. Bengalis may eat fish and still consider themselves vegetarians. In fact it's commonly believed that Bengalis simply can't live without fish, and they will go to any lengths to get it.

It seems reasonable that people who like fish this much will take the trouble to cook it well. Certain of Bengal's fresh-water fish present two problems to the cook. One of them is a muddy taste, and the other is bones. The taste is often corrected by soaking or washing in tamarind or lime juice, or rubbing with flour, ginger, or turmeric.

As for the bones—the Bengalis have worked out a cooking method that actually *melts* them. I know this sounds impossible, or outrageous to people who have learned that fish is best when cooked only until barely done. If you simmer a fish for 8 hours, which is the time it takes me to soften the bones in a fresh shad until they are as edible as the bones in a can of sardines or salmon, then won't the flesh turn into mush? Or if it holds together, won't it be a sort of tasteless cardboard? Well, in the

shad recipe in this section the fish holds together perfectly well, and it has plenty of taste. The texture is different from broiled or baked shad, but then it ought to be. It's a highly appetizing dish.

One final word about Indian spicing. Nobody much credits any more the old idea that curries are intended to cover up the taste of leftovers or inferior food. But many people still think that all Indian food is hot, or at least very spicy. Some is, but some isn't. Herbs and spices can be used with a bold hand in any style of cooking—for example, the pepper in French pepper steak, garlic in Spanish garlic soup, or ginger in American ginger snaps—and this tendency is admittedly more common in India than elsewhere. But India has many foods that are very delicately and subtlely seasoned. And there are many Indians who like *all* their foods without strong seasoning. Perhaps the reason more Indians like spices than not is that the results have a special intensity and appeal when the spices are of prime quality, fresh from the trees and vines where they grow.

African Peanut Soup

Not only peanuts, but fish, meat, and eggs all in one dish! Add a chicken if you want to. Needless to say, not all Africans are rich enough to live like this, but most Africans do make a lot of soups and stews with peanuts. Since they generally grind and pound them to a smooth paste, you can save time by using peanut butter.

 1 *pound lamb or beef, cut in small cubes*
 1 *pound salt cod, soaked overnight in cold water*
 1 *cup ground peanuts, or peanut butter*
 2 *cups canned Italian peeled tomatoes*
 2 *large onions, chopped*
 2 *small hot green chili peppers, diced, or cayenne pepper to taste*
 1 *pound okra*
 4 *hardcooked eggs*

As you see from the list of ingredients, this is a main-dish soup, not a first-course soup. Simmer the meat and fish together in 2 cups water for ½ hour. Remove fish, discard any skin and bones, and flake coarsely. Add all other ingredients except eggs to meat, and cook for another ½ hour or until meat is tender. Return fish to pot adding more water or not, depending on how thick you like your soup, and correct seasoning (salt from fish may well be enough). Serve in large soup plates, with a whole egg in the middle of each plate. *Makes 4 servings.*

Fried Chicken with Cashew Nut Sauce

1 frying chicken, disjointed
4 tablespoons peanut oil
½ cup ground cashew nuts
1 6-ounce can tomato paste

1 teaspoon salt
¼ teaspoon pepper
Dash of cayenne pepper

Fry chicken in oil until brown on all sides. Combine all other ingredients with 1½ cups warm water, add to pan, and simmer for 15 minutes or until chicken is tender. *Makes 2 to 4 servings, depending on accompaniments;* rice, okra, and fried bananas are favorites.

African Fish and Greens

1 large onion, chopped
4 tablespoons peanut oil
2 cloves garlic, minced
1 pound collards, kale, chard, or spinach
1 teaspoon salt
¼ teaspoon pepper
¼ teaspoon crushed red pepper, or cayenne to taste
1 pound solid fish, such as cod or haddock
2 tablespoons lemon juice

Sauté onion in oil until soft. Add garlic, greens, salt, and peppers, and cook until greens are just wilted, using only water that adheres to greens from washing, if possible. Chop greens. Add fish to greens and cook until it flakes easily. Flake it and mix through greens, together with lemon juice. Heat through. This goes well with baked yams. *Makes 4 servings.*

Lamb Tartare

If you eat raw beef, why not raw lamb? The success of this Arab dish depends on using the tenderest lamb you can get, cutting away all gristle, and grinding or pounding it as long as you have the strength.

> 2 *pounds loin lamb, or another tender lean cut*
> ½ *cup chopped onion*
> 1 *teaspoon salt*
> 2 *cups cracked wheat* (bulgur), *rinsed in water and pressed dry*
> *Olive oil*
> *Salt and pepper*

Trim the meat carefully and put through grinder with finest blade. Then grind again, together with onion and salt. Now grind a third time, adding cracked wheat. This should be the fine *bulgur*, not the coarse one, which is used to make pilaf. Now grind a fourth time with a sprinkle of ice water. If you aren't getting a smooth paste, start working the mixture with a pestle or pounding it with a mallet. The Arabs would have done it this way from the beginning, for at least an hour. When it is very smooth, spread it on a flat plate, sprinkle with olive oil, and add salt and pepper if you like. Chill for an hour or more. Bread and raw scallions or pickled turnips are good with this. *Makes 6 servings.*

Arab Lamb with Dates

2 *pounds lean lamb, cut in*
cubes
1 *large onion, chopped*
4 *tablespoons butter*
1 *tablespoon flour*
½ *teaspoon saffron, soaked*
in 2 tablespoons water

1 *stick cinnamon*
1 *teaspoon salt*
1 *cup dates, pitted and*
halved
1 *cup rice*
1 *teaspoon grated lemon*
rind

Sauté lamb and onion together in casserole with butter until meat loses its outside pink color and onion begins to soften. Sprinkle on flour, add all other ingredients except lemon rind, and stir for 3 minutes over high fire. Add 2½ cups water, cover, and cook slowly until water is absorbed and meat tender. Add lemon rind and heat through. Use more saffron if you feel extravagant. And if you like this dish as sweet and rich as the Arabs do, add a few spoons of sugar, and dribble on melted butter when you add the lemon rind. *Makes 6 servings.*

Biryani

Paella—Chinese fried rice—*nasi goreng*—*jambalaya*—which is the greatest rice dish of them all? The *richest* is certainly *biryani*, this heavenly pilaf of Pakistan and North India.

4 chopped onions
½ pound butter
2 tablespoons minced ginger
2 hot green chili peppers, minced
1 tablespoon curry powder
2 cloves garlic, minced
¼ cup blanched almonds, ground
1 Cornish game hen, disjointed
2 pounds lamb, cut in small cubes

1 pound rice
1 tablespoon salt
1 carton yogurt
2 tablespoons raisins
½ pint cream with 1 teaspoon saffron
2 tablespoons lime juice
¼ cup blanched almonds, whole
¼ cup chopped fresh coriander or mint
2 tablespoons rose water

Fry the onions in half the butter until golden. Add ginger, chili peppers, curry powder, garlic, ¼ cup ground almonds, game hen, lamb. Fry until game hen is browned. Meanwhile boil rice in 6 cups of water with salt for 15 minutes. Drain. Add yogurt to meat mixture, stir, and remove ⅔ of it from the pot. Cover the ⅓ left in the pot with ⅓ of the rice plus a few raisins. Now another layer of meat, rice, and raisins. Then the third and final layer of meat, rice, and raisins. Now pour on the remaining half of the butter, melted. Close pot and bake at 325° for 1 hour. Remove from oven and dribble on cream with saffron and lime juice, and garnish top with remaining half of almonds and coriander or mint. Return to oven, uncovered, for 15 minutes. Just before serving, sprinkle on rose water. *Makes 6 servings.*

Bombay Lobster

2 large onions, minced
1/4 pound butter
1 teaspoon turmeric
2 green chili peppers,
  minced

1 cup canned Italian peeled tomatoes
1½-pound lobster
1 teaspoon salt
2 tablespoons lime juice

Cook onions in butter until translucent. Add turmeric, peppers, and tomatoes, and cook 5 minutes more. Cut up lobster
with shell, separating the claws at the joints and cracking them,
and cutting across the tail in 1" widths. Add to pan, cover,
and cook about 7 minutes. Add salt and lime juice. The obvious
accompaniment is rice, but French bread is good too, or one of
the Indian or Arab breads, if you have the patience to make
them. *Makes 2 servings.*

Shrimps with Cucumber

1½ pounds shrimps
2 teaspoons turmeric
2 tablespoons vegetable oil
2 cucumbers, peeled,
  seeded and cubed
1 onion, sliced thin
1 hot green chili pepper,
  minced

1 clove garlic, minced
1 teaspoon salt
1 tablespoon minced gin-
  ger root (fresh)
1 tablespoon mustard seeds
1 cup buttermilk

Wash shrimps and steam with turmeric until they turn pink.
You don't need any more water than what clings to them from
the washing. Peel and de-vein. Fry together all other ingredients
except buttermilk. When onion begins to brown, add shrimps
and fry for 5 minutes more. Add buttermilk and cook slowly
for another 5 minutes. *Makes 4 servings.*

Baked Fish with Green Herbs

1 4-pound fish such as striped bass, sea bass or red snapper
1 cup cider vinegar
½ cup chopped green onions
½ cup chopped fresh coriander
2 hot green chili peppers, minced
2 tablespoons minced ginger
4 tablespoons vegetable oil
1 teaspoon cumin seeds

Marinate fish in vinegar for 12 hours, turning once or twice. Drain. Combine all remaining ingredients except oil and stuff in cavity of fish, which has first been rubbed with oil. Rub oil over outside of fish and place on double layer of aluminum foil. Dribble remaining oil over fish, fold and seal foil, and bake in 350° oven about 45 minutes, or until fish tests done. *Makes 4 servings.*

Fish Kebabs

2 pounds solid fish cut in large cubes
1 carton (½ pint) yogurt
2 cloves garlic, mashed
1 teaspoon paprika
1 teaspoon salt
1 tablespoon curry powder
¼ cup vegetable oil

To reduce the fishiness of fish, people in various parts of the world rub it with flour, then wash it off (the Indians would do this with dried pea flour), or wash it in water with garlic, or marinate it in vinegar, or use a little ginger or scallion in the cooking. None of these tacks is necessary when the fish is perfectly fresh, but often it isn't. Make this dish with swordfish, halibut, or any fish you can buy in a thick boneless piece. Marinate fish for 2 hours in combination of all remaining ingredients except oil. Place on skewers and grill until done, turning frequently and basting with oil. *Makes 4 servings.*

Poached Shad with Melted Bones

In eastern India and Burma they have a fish named *hilsa* which is delicious but full of small bones. Sometimes, to avoid coping with mouthfuls of bones or wasting half the fish by filleting it, they just cook it until the bones get soft enough to eat. I find that this works with one of my favorite springtime fish, shad.

1 4-pound shad, cleaned and head removed, but left whole	10 cloves garlic, minced
	1 tablespoon minced ginger root
1 teaspoon turmeric	2 hot green chili peppers
1 tablespoon salt	1 tablespoon mustard seeds
1 cup mild vinegar	½ cup vegetable oil
2 large onions, diced	

Rub fish with turmeric and salt, and let marinate in vinegar for several hours. Place in fish boiler with marinade. Add all other ingredients with water almost to cover, and simmer for 8 hours. In serving the fish you may wish to discard the large backbone, but the other bones should be as soft and edible as those in a can of salmon. *Makes 8 servings.*

Cod Roe and Green Bean Curry

Scandinavians eat lots of cod roe, but the fish markets in New York seem to have a hard time giving it away. You can make this Indian dish with any other kind of fresh roe you happen to find.

2 onions, sliced

3 tablespoons vegetable oil

1 clove garlic, minced

½ teaspoon minced ginger root

½ teaspoon turmeric

½ teaspoon cumin

1 teaspoon salt

2 tablespoons chopped coriander leaves

1 cup buttermilk

1 package frozen green beans

2 tablespoons lemon juice

1 teaspoon sugar

½ pound cod roe

Fry onions in 2 tablespoons oil until brown. Add garlic, ginger root, turmeric, cumin, salt, and coriander, and fry for 3 more minutes. Add buttermilk, bring to boil, and add beans. Cook covered for 5 minutes or until barely tender. Add lemon juice and sugar. In another skillet, sauté roe in 1 tablespoon oil for 2 to 4 minutes on each side, depending on size, then add to other ingredients and heat through. If fresh roe is unavailable, use canned roe—any kind. I have also made this dish with oysters in place of roe. *Makes 4 servings.*

Duck with Three Kinds of Onions

1 4½-pound duck, quar-
tered
½ cup chopped onion
2 tablespoons minced garlic
1 teaspoon ground black
pepper

2 teaspoons salt
1 cup mild vinegar, or ½
cup vinegar, ½ cup water
2 onions, sliced
4 green onions, minced

Put duck in casserole with all remaining ingredients except sliced and green onions. Turn to coat all surfaces with onion-vinegar mixture, then cover casserole and bake at 325° for 2 hours, turning once or twice. Lift duck quarters carefully from liquid and place under a low flame in the broiler for ½ hour or until all remaining fat is melted out and skin is very crisp. From top of liquid in casserole spoon off 2 tablespoons duck fat and fry sliced onions in this on a high fire until quite brown. Serve duck garnished with brown onions and raw scallions. *Makes 4 servings.* (Chill liquid in which duck cooked, discard fat, and use as sauce with rice or as stock.)

Carrot Halva

1 14-ounce can condensed
   milk
2 cups grated carrot
Sugar (optional)

1 cup melted butter
½ teaspoon saffron, soaked
   in 2 tablespoons hot milk
½ cup blanched almonds

Mix 1 cup of water with the milk. Add the carrot and cook until very tender, ½ hour or more. There is sweetening in the milk, but you can add sugar if you like a very sweet dessert. Indians sometimes make this *halva* from a variety of red-colored carrot which is so sweet that even they don't feel the need for more sweetening. Add the butter a little at a time, stirring and cooking. Add the saffron and half of the almonds, slivered. Use the remaining half of the almonds to garnish the plate of *halva*. Another attractive Indian garnish is edible silver or gold leaf. *Makes 6 servings.*

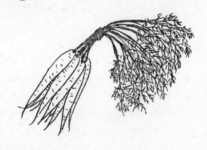

Indian Rice Pudding

½ pound rice
2 quarts milk
1 cup sugar
2 tablespoons raisins
2 tablespoons pistachios, chopped
½ teaspoon cardamom seeds (grains removed from pods)
½ teaspoon saffron, soaked in 2 tablespoons warm milk

Wash rice well and let it soak in cold water for 1 hour. Drain. Add to milk and simmer (don't allow to boil) for 1 hour. Add sugar, raisins, nuts, and cardamom, and simmer until rice is fully soft and pudding is as thick as you want it—as much as 2 or 3 hours more. Add saffron and allow to stand for at least 5 minutes before serving. This may also be eaten cold. *Makes 6 servings.*

SECTION FOUR

The Seas of China and Japan

THE SEAS OF CHINA AND JAPAN

Introduction

THE first time I ever tasted Chinese food was in London, in 1938, on my way to the United States. We spent only one evening there, but if our stay had been longer we might well have returned to the same Chinese restaurant every night, so interesting was the food. Today there are a few Chinese restaurants in Copenhagen, but I don't believe there were any then.

When Peter was a little boy, he and his brother Tom used to dig a hole in their back yard, making it a little deeper every day, convinced—like so many other little boys—that they would reach China if they just kept on digging. I don't suppose it was Chinese food that Peter was after at that time, but by the time I knew him he was certainly fond of Chinese dishes. In the 1940's and early 1950's we went very often to Chinese restaurants in New York, either by ourselves, or preferably with friends so that we could all taste a variety of dishes. Robert Flaherty, a great friend of Peter's, impressed us by ordering especially well from a Chinese menu.

Nobody we knew at that time thought of doing Chinese cooking at home—the restaurants did it so well. And they were so inexpensive. And it was supposed to be very difficult. And where could you find all the exotic ingredients?

I didn't know Japanese food in Denmark either. The first Japanese meal I had in New York impressed me deeply. The pretty arrangement on a lacquered tray, the artfully cut radishes and other vegetables in the clear soup—everything looked so beautiful. And the hot towels. At that time there were only two Japanese restaurants in New York, while today there are more than a dozen good ones.

I still often eat in Chinese and Japanese restaurants, but now it seems as though almost everyone is doing at least some Oriental cooking at home. Maybe not making lacquered ducks or serving raw fish, but at least cooking more vegetables the crisp Chinese way or using a bottle of teriyaki sauce at the outdoor barbecue. Of course there are some dishes better left to the professional chefs. On a short visit to Hong Kong a few years ago I was won over to great admiration for Peking Duck, but I still don't make it at home because it takes so long. (Incidentally, conditioned as I was by years of work for *Vogue*, I thought all the Chinese I saw on my visit to Hong Kong looked very stylish in their big coolie hats and black pajamas.)

Peter never visited the Far East—the closest he got was Siberia—but we knew people from everywhere at the United Nations and the Explorers Club. And he met Chinese sailors and cooks and merchants, on shipboard and ashore, practically everywhere. And there were the restaurants. We especially loved them for the wonderful things they do with fish. Whole steamed fish with different sauces, butterfly shrimps with bacon, fish with fermented black beans and garlic, shrimp toast—the possibilities seemed endless and always exotic. Peter only avoided the sweet and sour dishes (too sour for his taste) and the Chinese mustard (too hot). Two of his favorite dishes were Cantonese Lobster and Shrimps with Lobster Sauce. Neither is difficult to make, and I have given recipes for both in this section.

One of our favorite restaurants was a place on Lexington Avenue where they kept a tank of tropical fish near the door. Peter took a personal interest in the fish, saying he liked to drop in frequently to see how they were getting along. I think we ate there regularly enough so that he actually could keep track of them.

The year after Peter died I took a trip to Japan by myself.

The beauty of my first Japanese meal in New York was repeated and extended many times. And there were new facets too. I liked the papier maché models of food in the windows of the restaurants—real, functional pop art. During my stay in Tokyo I spent some weekends with friends at Misaki, a fishing village about fifty miles south of the city, at the tip of a peninsula. It was quite different from our own fishing village of Noank. The harbor was crowded with large boats full of tuna, each fish about five or six feet long—thousands and thousands of them. There were also some smaller fishing boats in which the fishermen appeared to be working in a funny position, bottoms up, like diving ducks.

I went to Kyoto at cherry blossom time, when the hotels were all so crowded there wasn't a room to be had. Friends arranged for me to stay in the private guest house of a great lady who had been a geisha. It was all terribly elegant, with servants on their knees and crouching in and out of the sliding doors all the time, and I slept in one of those Japanese envelopes of sheets and quilts on the floor. Nobody in the house understood a word of English, so whenever I wanted something I wrote it down on a piece of paper, an obliging servant took it out into the street and found someone who could translate it into Japanese, brought it back, and showed it around to the others, who all smiled and said "*hai, hai*," meaning "yes, yes, *now* we understand what she was driving at." The New York City Ballet was performing in Kyoto at the time I was there, and one day I gave a tea party for some friends from the company. My elegant hostess outdid herself in supplying the traditional, elaborate, and very colorful (though not very sweet or tasty) cookies and cakes that go with fine tea in Japan. I never quite adjusted to the bowl of bean soup they brought me every morning for breakfast, but as soon as I got out into the street I bought a small box of seaweed and munched it on my way to visit the temples and art collections of the great city.

No one else arranges food so carefully and exquisitely as the Japanese. Without overlooking the taste, their dishes are conceived at least half for appearance. Colors are harmonized and masses balanced as carefully as in the composition of a painting, and each shape has its own appropriately-shaped plate. In addition to appearance, meals are carefully planned for balance of tastes and textures. Everyone in Japan lives relatively close to the sea, and everyone eats fish—every kind of fish, cooked in every way, and best of all, raw. (They even enjoy one fish whose poison is fatal if it isn't handled in a certain precise way —a kind of culinary Russian roulette.) If you select raw fish carefully in the market and serve it with the knowledge and skill of the Japanese, it can bring a new dimension of gourmet dining into your life. In this section I've written something about each of the popular ways of serving it, as *sashimi* and as *sushi*.

It's true you have to go shopping for some special ingredients to do Oriental cooking (more of them are required for Japanese than for Chinese cooking; in fact there are many Chinese dishes you can do accurately and well with staples from the supermarket), or you can order them by mail. But once you have a basic supply, you can make these dishes over and over again for months without further trouble. Here are a few comments on the ones needed for my recipes.

Fresh ginger root, sold in Oriental and Puerto Rican groceries, will keep for several days as is, or you can peel and freeze it, then grate or slice what you need off the frozen root, which keeps for months.

Soy sauce, American-made and Japanese both sold in supermarkets, the latter mild but very good; or you can buy larger more economical sizes of Japanese soy sauce as well as the heavier darker soy sauce from Hong Kong in Oriental groceries.

Fermented black beans, fresh bean sprouts, sesame oil, all sold in Oriental groceries.

Canned water chestnuts, bamboo shoots sold in supermarkets, but more economical sizes in Oriental groceries. If whole, not sliced, both can be kept in covered jars in the refrigerator for 2 weeks if they are drained and covered with fresh cold water every other day.

Fish sauce, fish vinegar, Vietnamese *nuoc mam*—something

in this category (not the real sauce from Vietnam) will be available at Oriental groceries, most likely either Rufina *patis* from the Philippines or a fish soy sauce from Hong Kong. Probably nobody from one country would agree that the other country's fish sauce will do for his cuisine, but I find that any one of them gives you a good idea of the taste.

Wasabi powder, sold only in Japanese groceries, is a perfectly dry powder and will keep in its covered can for years.

Fresh white radish, fresh horseradish, sold in Oriental groceries.

Konbu and *nori* seaweed, both dried; Japanese rice vinegar; dried flaked *katsuobushi* or *bonito* (to make *dashi*); all sold only in Japanese groceries.

Mirin, sold at some liquor stores that handle sake, but by no means all; ask the Japanese grocer where to get it.

Sake is sold at many liquor stores. Different brands have somewhat different tastes, so compare them and make your choice. Always drink it warm (tepid, not boiling), little sips at a time. Some Japanese like to drink first, then eat; others drink and eat together. *Sake* is certainly the drink that tastes best with Japanese food, though cold beer is good too. If you drink *sake* you do not eat rice at the same time, traditionally, because *sake* is regarded as liquid rice. In any case rice is usually held back until the end of an elaborate Japanese dinner, when it is served with pickles and tea, more or less as a separate course.

Cantonese Lobster

4 1¼-pound lobsters
½ pound lean pork, ground
4 scallions, minced
1 teaspoon salt
4 slices ginger
4 tablespoons peanut oil

1 cup fish or chicken stock
2 tablespoons cornstarch
2 tablespoons soy sauce
4 tablespoons sherry
2 eggs, beaten

Cut up the lobsters by severing the spinal cord, cutting the tail in half lengthwise, then into 1-inch sections (shell and all), cutting each claw into 3 pieces, and cutting each head section into 4 pieces after removing the dark gritty sack. Use any legs large enough to be worth the trouble, but discard the smaller ones. Crack the hard shell of the claws so that you can pry the meat out without further cracking when it is cooked and covered with sauce. Sauté the pork, scallions, salt, and ginger in the oil for 2 minutes. Add lobster, stir and sauté until it is well mixed. Add stock, cover, and cook on medium heat for 10 minutes. Combine cornstarch, soy sauce, and sherry, adding any liquid you were able to catch when you cut up the lobsters, and stir this gradually into sauce with lobster. When sauce is thickened, add eggs, stir for 1 minute, and serve immediately. *Makes 6 main-dish servings, or more in combination with other Chinese dishes.*

Shrimps with Lobster Sauce

The sauce has no lobster in it, but is considered especially suited to lobster, so you might like to try it both ways. In fact the same sauce is used with Cantonese lobster, except that here I like to add black beans and garlic, in case the shrimps have an iodine taste that needs a bit of toning down. (Many Chinese restaurants add them with lobster too.)

1½ pounds shrimps, peeled and de-veined
2 tablespoons sherry
¼ pound lean pork, ground
1 tablespoon fermented black beans, washed clean of salt,
   crushed (obtainable at Chinese groceries)
2 cloves garlic, crushed
2 tablespoons peanut oil
1 tablespoon soy sauce
½ cup fish or chicken stock
2 scallions, cut in 1" pieces
1 tablespoon cornstarch
2 eggs, beaten

Marinate shrimps in sherry for 10 minutes. Sauté pork, beans, and garlic in oil for 2 minutes. Add shrimps and sauté until they turn pink. Add any remaining sherry marinade, soy sauce, and chicken stock, cover, and cook for 5 minutes. Add scallions and cornstarch (which has been dissolved in cold water or stock) a little at a time. When thickened, add eggs and stir for 1 minute. *Makes 4 servings.*

Steamed Sea Bass

1 2-pound sea bass	1 tablespoon soy sauce
1 teaspoon black beans,	1 tablespoon sherry
washed clean of salt	1 tablespoon peanut oil
1 teaspoon minced ginger	2 scallions, cut in 2" pieces

Combine all ingredients and rub inside of fish with some of the liquid. Place half the pieces of scallion inside, and place the rest of the scallion, together with the sauce, on top of the fish. Now put the fish on the rack of a fish-steamer or boiler, with just enough water in the bottom to make steam but not to boil up over the fish. You can protect the fish by putting it on a plate, if you have a long one that fits in the steamer, or on a double layer of aluminum foil. Bring water to a boil, cover pan, and steam for 15 minutes or until fish tests done. *Makes 2 servings.*

Chicken Salad with Bean Sprouts

Perhaps you'd like a change from chicken salad with mayonnaise, and you've temporarily had your fill of vinaigrette sauce too. This Chinese version* from Grace Zia Chu's fine book, *The Pleasures of Chinese Cooking*, is different, delicious, and even low in calories.

1 can bean sprouts or ½	1 teaspoon sesame-seed oil
pound fresh bean sprouts	½ teaspoon salt
1 chicken breast	½ teaspoon sugar
1 tablespoon soy sauce	¼ teaspoon monosodium
2 teaspoons wine vinegar	glutamate
1 teaspoon peanut oil	

Drain canned bean sprouts and soak them in cold water overnight. Or wash and blanch fresh bean sprouts. Simmer

* Reprinted by permission from *The Pleasures of Chinese Cooking* by Grace Zia Chu, © 1962, published by Simon and Schuster, Inc.

chicken breast until barely done and shred. Mix all other ingredients together in a bowl, and pour the mixture over the bean sprouts. Mix in chicken and chill. *Makes 2 to 4 servings.*

Peking Dust

In France they call this dessert Mont Blanc. If you can buy canned whole chestnuts (not preserved or glazed), or dried ones (in Italian and Spanish stores), you'll save the trouble of shelling and blanching the fresh ones.

1 pound chestnuts (or ½ pound dried chestnuts)
½ cup sugar
Pinch of salt
Whipped cream, sweetened and flavored with vanilla

Slash the shell of each chestnut on the flat side, boil for 1 minute, and remove from heat. Peel off shells and bitter brown inside skins, keeping nuts in warm water until each one is ready to be peeled (this helps skins come off more easily). Now cook the blanched nuts in water for 40 minutes, or until tender. Or soak dried chestnuts in water overnight, then simmer until they are swelled up and tender. Drain and put through a food mill or coarse sieve. Mix in sugar and salt. Now put through a ricer to make a light mound or peak, and cover the top with whipped cream. *Makes 6 servings.*

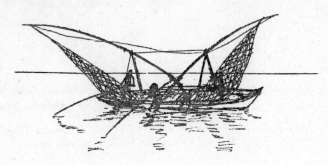

Chinese Glazed Fruit

Bananas cut in quarters (lengthwise, then across), large slices of apple with the peel left on, large orange sections with membrane intact, chunks of pineapple, kumquats—all can be glazed or candied the Chinese way. An elegant cousin of our popular jelly (candied) apple on a stick.

4 bananas, cut in quarters, or other fruits for 4 people
1 tablespoon peanut oil

¾ cup sugar
⅔ cup cider vinegar
2 tablespoons cornstarch
Pinch of salt

Sauté bananas or other fruit gently in oil and sprinkle with 1 tablespoon of the sugar. Combine the rest of sugar, cider vinegar, cornstarch, and salt in another pan and stir over medium heat until you have a smooth syrup. Boil for 2 minutes, then pour over fruit in first pan, heat and boil 2 minutes more. Using tongs, lift pieces of fruit out one at a time and hold in bowl of water with ice cubes until glazed coating hardens. *Makes 4 servings.*

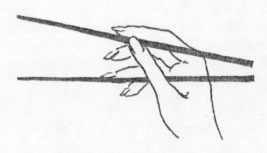

Korean Garlic Steak

My favorite way to cook a flank steak, this brings together the tastes Koreans like so well: garlic, sesame, and ginger.

1 flank steak, 2 to 3 pounds, well trimmed
2 tablespoons minced garlic
2 tablespoons sesame oil
1 tablespoon vinegar
1 tablespoon minced ginger
2 tablespoons sugar
4 tablespoons minced scallions
3 tablespoons soy sauce

Combine all ingredients except soy sauce, and marinate steak in them overnight in the refrigerator, or 4 hours at room temperature. If you don't have sesame oil, use vegetable oil plus 2 tablespoons ground sesame seeds. Add soy sauce just before broiling steak (long marinating in soy sauce can toughen meat, because of the high salt content). Broil on a hot fire only 3 minutes on each side, basting with any remaining marinade. Slice diagonally, as thin as possible. Very brief cooking and very thin diagonal slicing (closer to horizontal than vertical) keep flank steak tender. *Makes 6 servings.* Thin slices of this steak may also be threaded onto small bamboo skewers and served cold as appetizers.

Vietnamese Shellfish Omelet

This version of Chinese *eggs foo yong* uses whatever shellfish happen to be at hand—small shrimps, clams, oysters, mussels, scallops, crabmeat, lobster.

> 1 *pound shrimps, peeled, de-veined, and chopped*
> 1 *pound mussels, or 2 pounds clams, either small or chopped*
> 1 *pound bay scallops, or sea scallops chopped*
> ½ *cup diced water chestnuts*
> 4 *tablespoons minced shallot*
> 4 *tablespoons* nuoc mam (*or any fish sauce, such as* patis *from the Philippines*)
> 2 *hot green chili peppers, minced*
> 8 *eggs, beaten*
> ¾ *cup peanut oil*

Steam open shells of mussels or clams, remove meat and combine with all other ingredients except oil. Heat 2 tablespoons of oil in a skillet, spoon in ⅙ of the mixture, cover and cook until egg is set. Repeat 5 more times, keeping finished omelets warm in oven. These will not be brown, but they have a delicate texture and tenderness that is preferable. Serve with additional fish sauce, or soy sauce combined with vinegar, for dipping. *Makes 6 servings.*

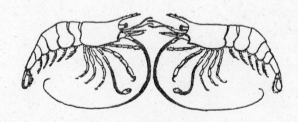

Sashimi

Your friends' amazement at being served raw tuna fish, lobster, or chicken may be kept in bounds if you remind them that they're quite used to eating raw oysters and clams—*live* raw oysters and clams, and at least these Japanese delicacies are decently deceased. The finest *sashimi* requires the freshest fish and the minimum of handling. As soon as fish is cut, bacteria begins to grow on the surface, so you'll do better to fillet your own smaller fish than to buy prepared fillets. And have the fish merchant cut you a block of fresh tuna to order; don't take a piece that's already cut. If you have doubts about bacteria, or if it makes you feel better, you can scald the fish. (Japanese do this too, but they recognize that it makes a different taste.) Dip pieces of lobster, chicken, etc., in and out of boiling water quickly. Or put a fillet on a cutting board set at an angle in the sink, cover it with cheesecloth, pour on a little boiling water, remove the cloth, rinse the fish in cold water, and dry it.

All *sashimi* should be cut into convenient bite-sized pieces. A small fillet is sliced clear across, at an angle to make 1-inch-wide slices, no more than ¼" thick. Larger fillets are first cut in half lengthwise. Tuna is cut into various shapes, cubes, batons, etc., but most often into slices about like the white fillets, only perhaps thicker. Japanese keep dipping their hands in cold water while cutting *sashimi* so that the delicate flavor of the fish won't be damaged by body heat. They also lift and move the fish with the knife, touching it as little as possible. Bones can be removed with tweezers.

Various vegetables, cut in very thin slices or delicate shreds, are served with *sashimi*, most frequently sweet white radish (in threads or grated), carrot, and cucumber. There's always a small dish of soy sauce, either plain or mixed with a little vinegar, lemon juice, or wine and *dashi*, the basic Japanese fish broth. You can vary its strength not only in the way you mix it, but also in the way you dip each bite of fish in it—half way in for a stronger taste, only a corner for the more delicate. A little grated fresh horseradish, or a paste made from powdered *wasabi*, a very strong radish, is almost always supplied to mix in the soy sauce. Paper-thin slices of fresh ginger are also popular.

The presentation of *sashimi* on special plates or trays is an art something like flower arrangement. A former chef at New York's Nippon Restaurant used to carve blocks of ice to use as trays—shaped like a swan, a whale, a basket—and cut dark red tuna and white striped bass into thin slices that he formed into the petals of red and white roses. You can make a whole landscape out of raw fish if you feel like it. On the other hand, a row of simple slices on a pretty plate with a bit of *wasabi* and soy sauce are enough.

Fresh tuna and striped bass are the most popular fish for *sashimi* where I live, but almost any salt-water fish or shellfish can be used. Here are directions for preparing two of the more unusual types.

Lobster Sashimi

2 1-pound lobsters
½ cup shredded white radish or cucumber
3 tablespoons Japanese soy sauce
1 teaspoon lemon juice
Dash of monosodium glutamate
Grated fresh horseradish, or paste prepared from wasabi powder and water

Separate the head and tail sections of live lobsters. Remove meat carefully from the tails and boil shells until red. Chill. Cut meat into ¼″ slices and chill in ice water for 10 minutes. Remove, dry, and keep cold. Line shells with shredded white radish, cucumber, or any vegetable that pleases you (a touch of bright green is nice). Arrange slices of lobster on top. Serve with sauce made from soy, lemon juice, and monosodium glutamate. The horseradish or *wasabi* paste is served separately so that each person may add only as much of it as he likes to the sauce. *Makes 2 servings*.

Chicken Sashimi

When you skin and bone raw breasts of chicken, you find that there is an inner piece of meat on each side, lying right next to the breast bone, which separates from the rest of the breast. These are the tenderest parts of the breast, and the parts preferred for *sashimi* if you really want to be a Japanese gourmet.

4 chicken breasts (8 halves), inner sections only
1 cucumber, cut in paper-thin slices
1" piece of ginger root, cut in paper-thin slices
Grated fresh horseradish, or wasabi paste
6 tablespoons Japanese soy sauce

Dip breast sections quickly in and out of boiling water. Dry, cool, and slice thin. Arrange on small plates with cucumber, ginger, and mounds of horseradish or *wasabi* paste. Serve small dishes of soy sauce separately, and mix horseradish into soy sauce before dipping in bites of chicken. *Makes 4 servings*.

Sushi

Sushi is so popular in Japan that there are many restaurants specializing in it, and many Japanese have a large lacquer box of *sushi* sent in from one of them rather than fixing it at home. (That way they can have more different kinds, without the trouble of shopping for small amounts of many different fish—which must all be of the best quality.) You can use any fish you would use for *sashimi*, either raw or cooked, as well as eggs, seaweed, pickles, and various vegetables. The idea is to cook vinegar-flavored rice so that the grains will stick together; then

make bite-size mounds of this, and cover each mound with a slice of fish or shellfish or omelet cut to fit. Or roll the rice in a sheet of *nori* seaweed with a center filling of pickle or fish. You eat *sushi* with your fingers, not chopsticks.

Sushi rice is cooked with relatively little water so that it does not get mushy. The Japanese recommend washing it to remove starch, then draining for 2 or 3 hours. Boil it the minimum time and in the minimum water—only a little bit more water than rice if you can get it tender that way, say 2¼ cups of water to 2 cups of rice. You can add a piece of *konbu* seaweed (the kind used in making *dashi*) when boiling up the water, but remove it before putting in the rice. You can also substitute for same amount of water, ¼ cup of *mirin*, the Japanese sweet white wine, if you like.

As soon as the rice is cooked, spread it out in a shallow pan, cool it quickly by fanning (use an electric fan if it's handy), at the same time stirring in a mixture of Japanese rice vinegar or white vinegar, sugar, and salt. For 6 cups of cooked rice, dissolve 2 tablespoons sugar and 2 tablespoons salt in ⅔ cup vinegar. Or use Japanese sweet rice vinegar. Add more vinegar if you like it and if the rice will absorb it.

Now press together a mound of rice about 2″ x 1″ x 1″ in the palm of one hand, add a touch of *wasabi* paste if you like it, and cover the top with a slice of raw tuna or half a parboiled shrimp or a slice of rather stiff cold omelet. (This is also a good way to enjoy such familiar American delicacies as raw oysters and clams, smoked salmon, and red caviar—but in the latter case, better leave the salt out of the rice.) Serve with a small dish of soy sauce for dipping.

Sometimes the Japanese make fancy decorated *sushi* that remind me of Danish open-faced sandwiches. Sometimes they wrap it up in surprise packages that look like one thing but turn out to be something else. And often they pack it into the world's most elegant lunch boxes. But the basic bite-sized mounds described above are the most popular way to serve it. How many of them a *sushi*-lover can devour I've never discovered, but you ought to figure on at least 8 or 10 for each of your guests.

Broiled Fish
(*Teriyaki*)

Other foods can be broiled with this same sauce—beef and pork are both very good—and the sauce can be stored in a jar in the refrigerator for repeated use. Just add a little more of each ingredient to the jar each time you use some up, and keep it going like a Spanish sherry *solera*.

5 *fish fillets*	½ *cup soy sauce*
½ *cup* dashi *(see Note below)*	½ *cup* mirin *or sweetened* sake

Use any fairly thick fillets or fish steaks—fresh tuna, striped bass, mackerel, salmon, swordfish. Since the Japanese like things in sets of five, we'll say five of them—the idea is one for each person. Marinate the fish in the sauce made from *dashi*, soy sauce and *mirin* for ½ hour. If you have trouble getting *mirin*, use *sake* (or in a pinch, sherry) and 2 tablespoons of sugar. Broil carefully, about 10 minutes, on one or both sides (depending on thickness and distance from heat), basting with a little of the sauce 3 or 4 times. If you are broiling on skewers, you can dip the fish in the sauce each time you turn it. Serve sprinkled with a few drops of warmed sauce, or with small side dishes of warmed soy sauce and lemon juice, half and half. *Makes 5 servings.*

NOTE: To make basic *dashi*, place a small piece of *konbu* seaweed (about 1″ square, washed) in 2 cups of water and bring to a boil. Remove seaweed, add ⅓ cup flaked *katsuobushi*, let steep for 2 minutes and strain. Add 1 teaspoon salt and ½ teaspoon soy sauce. This is the strong *dashi* to use for sauces and soups. For *chawanmushi* and certain other mild-flavored dishes, a second weaker *dashi* is made by steeping the same seaweed and *katsuobushi* over again, plus a little fresh *katsuobushi*, and omitting the salt and soy sauce. *Dashi* is Japan's basic stock.

Broiled Chicken on Skewers
(Yakitori)

If you own a *hibachi*, if you cook outdoors in the summer, if you have any means of doing charcoal broiling, these dainty bites of chicken are an ideal accompaniment to cocktails. The sauce is similar to the preceding *teriyaki* sauce but thicker.

1 broiling chicken, boned and cut in small bite-sized pieces
½ pound additional chicken livers, cut bite-sized
8 scallions, cut in 1½" lengths
¾ cup soy sauce
¾ cup mirin, or sake plus 2 tablespoons sugar
Cayenne pepper

Thread chicken onto small Japanese bamboo skewers, alternating light and dark meat or chicken meat and liver, or chicken and scallion—about 4 pieces of meat to a skewer. Dip into sauce which has been made by boiling up soy sauce and *mirin* (or *sake* with sugar), or use leftover *teriyaki* sauce. Broil quickly, turning and dipping back in sauce every minute or two. Do not overcook or the meat will dry out. Dust with cayenne. *Makes 15 or more skewers.*

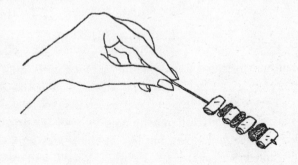

145

Broiled Eels

This is one more use for the basic *teriyaki* sauce, except that here the sauce may have some eel broth or stock in place of *dashi*. Eels are so popular in Japan that there are restaurants that serve nothing else. There they usually cut up the live eel before your eyes (and I also saw this done once at the *Sushi* bar of a New York restaurant, where several of the American customers coudn't quite believe what was happening), fillet the body for broiling, and make a bouillon of the bones and head. Part of the broth goes into the sauce, while part may be served to you in a soup bowl with the eel's giblets, and a garnish of some sculptured vegetable. Cut the eel fillets in convenient lengths, about 3″ or 4″, and skewer them crosswise on bamboo sticks. Dip them in sauce and broil on hot fire. Paint them with the sauce several times during the broiling, and keep a fan handy to put out the flash fires from dripping fat. Dust with cayenne and serve with plain boiled rice. Eels cooked this way are so good that even your non-eel-loving friends may be won over.

Egg Custard
(Chawanmushi)

This delicate egg custard makes either a first course at an American dinner or one of half a dozen dishes at a Japanese dinner— not a dessert (it's not sweet). You can put in more or less ingredients, including fresh mushrooms as well as dried, water chestnuts, gingko nuts, pork in place of chicken, fish fillet, *kamaboko* (steamed fish cake, very brightly colored), and green peas. Japanese usually serve a thin slice of fresh citron or lemon with it.

146

2 *cups* dashi, *or very mild fish stock*
1 *raw chicken breast, skinned and boned, cut in 8 pieces*
4 *raw shrimps, peeled and de-veined*
Sake
4 *dried mushrooms, soaked and boiled in* dashi *with soy sauce*
3 *eggs*
2 *tablespoons Japanese soy sauce*
Monosodium glutamate
4 *small slices bamboo shoots*
4 *sprigs of watercress or small leaves of spinach*

The mild *dashi* used here is made from only the shavings of dried *bonito* and *konbu* seaweed. (See p. 144 for making *dashi*. You can buy a new powder for instant *dashi* under such trade names as Hi-me and Yamasa Flave.) Steam the pieces of chicken breast and the shrimps over the *dashi* for 5 minutes. Allow *dashi* to cool. Sprinkle *sake* over chicken, shrimps, and mushrooms. Beat eggs, add *dashi* and soy sauce, and put through fine strainer. Add a dash or two of monosodium glutamate. Now divide chicken, shrimps, mushrooms, and bamboo shoots equally between 4 custard cups or small bowls, pour the egg mixture over them, and place a sprig of watercress or small leaves of spinach on top. Cover bowls with lids or aluminum foil and set in a pan of boiling water that comes half way up their sides. Cover pan and steam for 10 minutes or more—until custard tests done with a sharp knife. Don't be too distressed if the custard separates; the Japanese classify this dish as a soup. *Makes 4 servings.*

Cucumber and Crab Salad

Fresh crab meat from the blue crabs of the eastern United States has a superb flavor, but I'll admit it's tiresome to pick over for bits of shell or cartilage. And after you do it carefully, it's even more tiresome to find some bits between your teeth when you bite down on the finished dish. Happily, this salad offers a way out. Eating it with chopsticks, virtually a flake at a time, you and your guests can do your final picking over at the table. Tell them it's an old Japanese custom to savor tiny bites of crab and examine each one for the glint of cartilage. You can also avoid the problem by substituting blanched bay scallops.

1 *pound fresh crab meat*	1 *tablespoon soy sauce*
2 *small cucumbers*	1 *teaspoon sugar*
Salt	*Monosodium glutamate*
3 *tablespoons Japanese*	*Fresh ginger cut in threads*
vinegar or lemon juice	*or thin strips*

Pick over the crab meat, removing cartilage. Peel and seed the cucumbers, slice very thin, salt and let stand for 15 minutes. Squeeze out moisture and sprinkle with 1 tablespoon vinegar. Mix remaining 2 tablespoons vinegar, soy sauce, sugar, and a dash of monosodium glutamate, and pour this over the crab. Arrange separate mounds of crab and cucumber on small plates, and garnish the cucumber with threads of ginger. *Makes 4 servings.*

Baked Eggplant

The Japanese would broil or fry the eggplant because they don't generally have ovens, but I find this works best (and cooks with less oil) in the oven.

1 *large eggplant cut in 6 thick slices, peeled*	4 *tablespoons soy sauce*
2 *tablespoons vegetable oil*	2 *tablespoons* mirin
4 *tablespoons peanut butter*	*Cayenne pepper*

Combine oil, peanut butter, soy sauce, and *mirin*, and spread over all surfaces of eggplant slices. Place slices on cooky sheet or any flat ovenproof dish and bake at 400° until tender, about ¾ hour. Sprinkle generously with cayenne. *Makes 6 servings.*

Spinach with Sesame and Seaweed

The Japanese way of living carefully, neatly, without waste is well illustrated by their methods for cooking spinach. One way is to pick up the washed spinach leaves by the stems and dip them in boiling salted water, a handful at a time, just until they wilt. Another is to pile the leaves in precise stacks in a pan, pour boiling water over them, and cook until wilted. In either case the leaves are then rinsed in cold water and all moisture is pressed or wrung out of them. Then the compressed spinach is cut in lengths of about 1 inch (uncooked stems are discarded) and served cold with a sauce, which may be just plain soy, or something more complicated like this.

1 pound spinach, cooked and cooled	2 tablespoons soy sauce
3 tablespoons sesame seeds	½ teaspoon sugar
	4 sheets nori seaweed

Toast the seeds in a dry pan until they color slightly. Crush in mortar and mix with soy sauce and sugar. Pour over spinach. Cut seaweed into squares of about 2″ and toast each one lightly over flame. Roll up a bit of the seasoned spinach in each square of seaweed as you eat it—a trick you can accomplish with chopsticks, given a little practice. *Makes 4 servings.*

SECTION FIVE

The South Seas

THE SOUTH SEAS

Introduction

ETER was one of those people who love islands, no matter what size or what kind. The most distant and most romantic have always been the islands of the South Seas. They were so isolated that it took many months to reach the area by ship. Then if you stopped off on one island you might have to wait several months for a ship to take you on to the next one. You really had to be a beachcomber to afford the time. Today this has changed, and Pan American Airways will fly you from the West Coast to Tahiti in eight hours. But the South Pacific is still relatively isolated and almost empty.

Men who stake their lives against and match wits with the sea face some of the same problems everywhere; but on the whole, life in the tropical South Seas is very different from life in the Arctic. One setting forces men to use all their strength and cunning just to survive—and many fail. The other makes survival a matter of reaching up to the trees for fruit and into the lagoon for fish. Here the problem is to take life seriously and remember to get some work done. I knew this feeling even on a brief visit to Hawaii—those lush beautiful islands where Polynesia begins but where the life is well over half-Americanized.

Polynesian cooking relies heavily on fish, fruits, and vegetables. With no pasturage to speak of, meat is scarce. And there's little use of fats. Seasoning is mild. Much of the "Polynesian" food served in American restaurants is really Chinese.

Sometimes it's very good Chinese food, and you might even find something much like it in the islands of the South Seas because there are many Chinese scattered among the islands. But it isn't real Polynesian food, and in this section I have tried to give some typical dishes that are.

The Maoris of New Zealand are a Polynesian people, and their islands mark the southern limit of the area. The cooking of both New Zealand and its island-continent neighbor, Australia, is of course more English-influenced than anything else, but I touch on it here for geographical reasons.

More important than the lands down under, both numerically and gastronomically, are the 3,000 islands of Indonesia, the 7,000 islands of the Philippines, and the neighboring countries of Southeast Asia. All of these could be grouped for culinary purposes with China. Some could also be grouped with India. But partly for balance, and partly because there's something distinctive about islands, I have put them together here. Neither of us ever visited any of them, though again we had contacts at the United Nations (where Peter always admired the ladies of the Philippines in their fairy-tale butterfly-sleeve dresses), and friends of ours brought back a cook from the Spice Islands who gave us many fine Indonesian dishes at their home. This cook was actually a Bulgarian dance instructor, Botjo Markoff, who had run a restaurant in Djakarta. His meals in our friends' house, which was a converted church in Stonington, Connecticut, were sometimes authentic Indonesian, sometimes just exotic—like the house.

Ingredients are not a major problem here. If you don't want to crack and scrape fresh coconuts to make coconut milk, look for unsweetened shredded coconut in supermarkets or health food stores. Make thick coconut milk by steeping the shredded coconut in warm water or milk, about 2 cups of coconut to 1 cup of liquid, for ½ hour; then squeeze through a cheesecloth. Use the same shreds over again to make thin milk, by pouring another cup (or more) of either water or milk over them—the more liquid, the thinner the milk—again steeping for ½ hour and squeezing dry. Discard the shredded coconut.

You can also give coconut flavor to a dish by grinding or pounding some toasted Hawaiian coconut chips and mixing them in, but people who live where the coconuts grow usually prefer to extract the flavor from the meat and discard the scrapings. I agree that a mouthful of coconut shreds from a stew that has cooked for some time can give you the impression you're chewing on tasteless bits of rope. (In fact the fibers of coconut husks make excellent matting that wears forever.)

If you make thick coconut milk with whipping cream, incidentally, you can still whip it (after chilling) and have delicious coconut-flavored whipped cream.

I've written notes about shrimp and fish sauces and pastes at the end of the Shrimp Sate recipe that follows and in the Introduction to Section 4. It's really worth the trouble to get one or two of these, but if you're caught short and want to go ahead with what's available at the supermarket, try anchovy paste and a little vinegar.

If you think peanut butter is for children, not for adults, and certainly not for your gourmet friends, then grind whole peanuts whenever a recipe calls for peanut butter. But I think you will find that no one is aware of eating peanut butter once it is mixed with red pepper, soy sauce, garlic, coconut milk, and other strong flavors.

If you have easy access to a Chinese grocery, by all means take advantage of it for *fresh* bean sprouts and *fresh* water chestnuts, which are certainly better than canned.

For petals from roses that have not been sprayed, I guess you'll have to look for wild roses or trust your own garden.

Coconut Marinated Fish

Scandinavians eat so much pickled fish that we feel right at home with Mexican *seviche* and with the marinated fish of Polynesia. Use any fresh ocean fish in the recipe that follows. It's a fair amount of trouble to open and grate a coconut in order to make coconut milk; the labor is much reduced if you can find unsweetened grated coconut in your grocery or health food store (not coconut for baking, which is always sweetened).

1 *pound striped bass, or other ocean fish, cut bite-sized*	½ *cup fresh lime juice*
	½ *cup thick coconut milk**
1 *clove garlic, minced*	*Salt and pepper*
1 *small onion, sliced thin*	

Combine first 4 ingredients and marinate for 1 hour at room temperature. Drain, discarding garlic and onion or not as desired. Add coconut milk and a sprinkle of salt and pepper to taste. Chill at least 1 hour in refrigerator. *Makes 4 appetizer servings.*

*Thick milk is the first pressing from grated coconut, not the milk you may find inside the coconut. See Introduction to this section.

Fish Packages
(*Laulau*)

A *laulau* is a little package of food wrapped up in *ti* leaves and steamed. If *ti* leaves are in short supply in your community and your kitchen doesn't have a steamer, the following recipe works just as well with aluminum foil and an oven.

1 *pound fresh spinach leaves*	1 *cup coconut milk*
2 *pounds fillets of flounder or sole*	*Salt and pepper*

Tear off six large squares of aluminum foil. Divide the spinach leaves (well washed) into six equal portions and place on squares of foil. Add fish fillets, again divided equally. Sprinkle each portion with coconut milk, salt, and pepper. Fold up foil and roll or crimp the edges so that no steam will escape. Bake in 375° oven for 45 minutes. *Makes 6 servings.*

Charcoal Broiled Red Snapper

This recipe is for a 2-pound fish, but you can cook a larger snapper or other kinds of fish in the same way, only adjusting the seasoning and cooking time according to size. Although charcoal broiled is my favorite, you can also cook in a broiler.

1 *2-pound red snapper*
2 *tablespoons vegetable oil*
1 *teaspoon minced ginger root, or* ½ *teaspoon powdered
    ginger*
Salt

Use the whole fish, head and tail left on. Rub with oil and ginger, making sure some of the ginger stays in the cavity. Place fish on its side on oiled grill over hot charcoal and broil for 10 minutes. Turn over carefully and broil until flesh near backbone tests done. Salt to taste. *Makes 2 servings.*

Coconut Spinach

2 *packages frozen spinach*
½ *cup coconut milk*
2 *tablespoons vegetable oil*
Salt and pepper
¼ *cup minced scallions*
¼ *cup crushed Hawaiian coconut chips (canned)*

Cook spinach with coconut milk in place of water. Add oil, plus salt and pepper to taste. Serve garnished with raw scallions and coconut chips. *Makes 6 servings.*

Shrimp Sate

A major problem in broiling shrimps, it seems to me, is their tendency to get dry. These Indonesian skewers (which can be made equally well with fish or any kind of meat, cut bite-sized) take care of that by marinating and by repeated dipping in the marinade during broiling.

1 *pound small shrimps, peeled and de-veined*	2 *tablespoons* patis (*see Note below*)
¼ *cup coconut milk*	2 *cloves garlic, minced*
2 *tablespoons soy sauce*	1 *teaspoon curry powder*
2 *teaspoons brown sugar*	2 *tablespoons peanut butter*
¼ *teaspoon crushed red pepper*	

Combine all ingredients except peanut butter and marinate for 1 hour at room temperature. Thread shrimps on small bamboo skewers (available at Oriental groceries and curio shops) and broil over hot charcoal or in a high broiler, turning frequently. Dip in marinade each time you turn the skewer. Add peanut butter to leftover marinade, heat and stir until it dissolves, and serve as sauce with skewers. *Makes 4 appetizer servings.*

NOTE: Many Indonesian dishes (and dishes from all other countries of Southeast Asia) call for a seasoning of one of the strong shrimp or fish sauces or pastes. The favorite in Indonesia is a shrimp paste called *trassi udang*. But the easiest to find (in Oriental groceries) is a sauce from the Philippines called Rufina *patis*. Chinese groceries also carry a canned shrimp paste.

Vegetables with Peanut Sauce
(Gadogado)

This is a dish of boiled, blanched, and raw vegetables with a spicy Indonesian peanut sauce—a good companion for fried, crisp, or otherwise rich foods. You can vary the choice of vegetables to suit your fancy. Also you can serve them hot, lukewarm, or cold, and oddly enough, it doesn't seem to make much difference.

1 can bean sprouts, heated in their juice, then drained
1 large cucumber, seeded and cut in bite-sized wedges
1 large green pepper, cut bite-sized
6 small new potatoes, boiled in jackets and halved
1 bunch large red radishes, halved
1 cup cooked green beans
6 tablespoons peanut butter
1 teaspoon crushed red pepper
2 tablespoons patis, or shrimp paste to taste
2 teaspoons brown sugar
1 clove garlic, minced
2 tablespoons lemon juice
Grated rind of 1 lemon

Arrange first 6 ingredients (or other vegetables) on large platter. To make sauce, combine next 5 ingredients with 1 cup water, heat and stir until peanut butter is fully dissolved, then simmer 5 minutes. (You'll be surprised how much the seasonings change the taste of peanut butter.) Add lemon juice and rind to sauce and serve with vegetables. Each person helps himself to each vegetable (omitting any that he never learned to like), and to as much or as little of the hot sauce as he wants. *Makes 6 servings.*

Indonesian Fried Rice
(*Nasi Goreng*)

This Indonesian version of **Chinese** fried rice can contain bits of almost any meat you want to put in. Make sure the boiled rice is fully cold before frying, or it will get sticky.

2 *large onions, chopped*
¼ *cup vegetable oil*
4 *cups cooked rice*
1 *cup cooked chicken, diced or shredded*
½ *cup diced Smithfield ham*
½ *pound small shrimps, shelled and de-veined*
½ *teaspoon crushed red pepper*
2 *tablespoons* patis (*see Note under Shrimp Sate*)
2 *tablespoons soy sauce*
1 *tablespoon ground coriander*
1 *teaspoon cuminseed*
2 *cloves garlic, minced*
2 *eggs, beaten*

Sauté onions in oil until translucent. Add **rice and fry** until well heated, turning constantly so that grains are **coated quickly** with oil. Add all other ingredients except garlic and **eggs;** stir and fry until shrimps turn pink. Add garlic, mix, and **remove** to warm platter. Make a thin omelet of the eggs, cut in strips, and place on top of rice. *Makes 4 servings.*

Noodles
(Bahmi)

The words *bah* and *mi* mean "*pork*" and "*noodles*." You can make this Chinese-Indonesian dish with fine egg noodles, thin spaghetti, linguini, fresh fettucine—almost any pasta that is cut fairly thin. As with fried rice, the ingredients vary according to what's available and what you like.

1 *pound pork, cut in small cubes without gristle but may have some fat (as from pork chops)*
2 *tablespoons vegetable oil*
3 *large onions, chopped*
1 *pound small shrimps, peeled and de-veined*
¼ *cup* patis
¼ *cup soy sauce*
1 *tablespoon brown sugar*
½ *teaspoon crushed red pepper*
1 *tablespoon paprika*
1 *small head Chinese celery cabbage, coarsely shredded*
4 *cloves garlic, minced*
1 *pound noodles, boiled until barely done, drained*
6 *scallions, chopped*

Sauté the pork in oil until browned and cooked through. Add onions and cook until translucent. Add next 6 ingredients and cook until shrimps are pink. Add celery cabbage and garlic, and cook just until cabbage is wilted. Add noodles, mix well, and keep on low heat until well heated through. Garnish each plate of noodles with raw scallions. *Makes 6 servings.*

Indonesian Lamb Curry

2 *pounds boneless lamb,*
cut in large cubes
¼ *cup vegetable oil*
1 *large onion, chopped*
1 *tablespoon curry powder*

1 *tablespoon ground cori-*
ander
4 *cloves garlic*
Grated rind of 1 lemon
2 *cups coconut milk*
2 *teaspoons salt*

Brown lamb in oil. Add next 3 ingredients and fry for 5 minutes. Add remaining ingredients, cover, and cook for 1 hour or until meat is tender. This curry will be mild or hot depending on your choice of curry powder, and you can add hot peppers if you like. *Makes 6 servings.*

Shrimp and Watercress Soup

This lovely soup from Burma is very strong with black pepper, but if you don't like so much black pepper just reduce the amount to suit your palate. Sesame oil can be bought from Oriental groceries and some health food stores.

1 *large onion, sliced thin*
2 *tablespoons sesame oil*
4 *cloves garlic, sliced*
2 *tablespoons patis (see Note under Shrimp Sate)*
1 *bunch watercress, coarsely chopped*
½ *pound shrimps, peeled, de-veined, and chopped*
Shells from shrimps
1 *teaspoon coarsely ground black pepper*
Salt

Fry onion in oil until golden. Add 4 cups water and all remaining ingredients except pepper and salt. Cover and simmer until watercress is tender. Remove shells. Add pepper and simmer 2 minutes. Add salt to taste. *Makes 6 servings.*

Spiced Meat Stew

Here is a very different type of curry from Southeast Asia, closer to what the Indonesians call a *gulai.*

2 *pounds boneless lamb,*	½ *teaspoon nutmeg*
cut in small cubes, well	¼ *teaspoon ground clove*
trimmed	2 *small sticks cinnamon*
1 *teaspoon monosodium*	½ *teaspoon ground car-*
glutamate	*damom*
¼ *cup vegetable oil*	1 *teaspoon minced ginger*
¼ *pound almonds,*	*root*
peeled and ground	½ *cup coconut milk*
½ *teaspoon black pepper*	*Salt*

The meat should be trimmed of all gristle and tough membrane and cut in bite-sized pieces, then sprinkled with monosodium glutamate. Fry it quickly in the oil, stirring constantly, until brown on all sides. Remove to cold plate. Add all other ingredients except salt to pan with oil and cook for 5 minutes or until well blended. Return meat to pan mixing it with other ingredients. Heat through, and add salt to taste. *Makes 6 servings.*

Rolled Stuffed Beef
(Morcon)

This Philippine stuffed beef roll requires thin sheets of lean meat such as Italian butchers prepare for *braciola* or *scaloppine.* If you have to do it yourself, pound thin-cut round or flank steak until it is only ¼" thick.

2 pounds beef steak in large thin slices
2 cloves garlic, minced
2 tablespoons soy sauce
2 tablespoons lemon juice
¼ teaspoon cayenne pepper
½ pound Smithfield ham, cut in thin strips

2 hardboiled eggs, quartered
¼ cup diced salt pork
2 tablespoons raisins
¼ cup chopped green olives
1 large onion, sliced
½ cup vinegar

Spread out the slices of meat end to end and sprinkle with garlic, soy, lemon juice, and cayenne. Arrange strips of ham and eggs side by side on top of beef slices, sprinkle on salt pork, raisins, and olives evenly, and roll up carefully, tucking in the ends so that stuffing will not fall out. Tie with string in both directions. Place in pan with onion, vinegar, and enough water to come at least half way up the side of the roll. Cover and simmer for 1 hour, turn over, and simmer for another hour. Remove from liquid, remove string, and slice crosswise with sharp knife. *Makes 6 servings.* If you like, you may thicken the liquid with cornstarch (correcting the seasoning) and serve as a sauce with the beef roll.

Baked Fish with Roe Soufflé

Because this recipe comes from Southeast Asia it calls for such indigenous seasonings as sesame oil, soy sauce, and coconut milk. But I suspect the same preparation is equally native to North America and Europe, without the exotic touches. If you can't get fresh fish roe, use red caviar from a glass jar (only making allowance for the salt in the caviar and choosing salmon steaks as the fish), or substitute a duxelles of mushrooms.

2 shallots, minced	1½ pounds fish fillets or
1 clove garlic, minced	steaks
2 tablespoons sesame oil	2 tablespoons soy sauce
½ pound fresh fish roe	¼ cup coconut milk
Salt	2 egg yolks and 3 egg
	whites, beaten separately

Sauté shallots and garlic in oil until they begin to brown. Add roe and sauté on both sides until cooked through. Add salt to taste. Crumble roe and cool. Place fish fillets or steaks in greased baking dish, sprinkle with soy sauce and coconut milk. Bake in 400° oven for 10 minutes. To finish the soufflé, mash roe mixture with fork and combine with 2 beaten egg yolks. Fold in whites and place evenly on top of fish. Return to oven and bake until done. *Makes 4 servings.*

Liver and Onions

Perhaps you need the finest calves liver if you're only going to sauté it in sweet butter. Maybe even for the delicious *Fegato alla Veneziana* you should choose the mildest-tasting raw material. But for this spicy Asian version of what seems to be a truly international dish, you may use steer, lamb, or pig's liver with equal confidence. (Peter liked pork liver the best, and I like it too because it has less membrane.) Just trim away any membrane as you cut it into bite-sized cubes. Note that it gets cooked the minimum length of time.

2 *large onions, sliced*	½ *teaspoon ground tur-*
4 *tablespoons sesame oil*	*meric*
2 *tablespoons* patis	½ *teaspoon crushed red*
2 *tablespoons soy sauce*	*pepper*
1 *tablespoon lemon juice*	1½ *pounds liver, cubed*

Fry onions slowly in half the oil until dark brown; this should take ½ hour or more. While onions are cooking, combine all remaining ingredients except oil and let marinate. Remove onions from pan, add remaining oil, and fry marinated liver quickly over high heat. Stop cooking as soon as brown on all sides; the liver should still be pink and juicy inside. Serve garnished with the browned onions. *Makes 4 servings.*

Burmese Duck

1 4½-*pound duck, accessible fat removed*
5 *cloves garlic, crushed*
1 *teaspoon ground ginger*
½ *cup* patis
2 *teaspoons monosodium glutamate*
2 *ounces dried mushrooms, washed thoroughly*
1 *tablespoon black pepper*
1 *cup sliced bamboo shoots*
5 *scallions, chopped*
1 *large tomato, sliced thin*
1 *large green pepper, seeded and sliced in thin rings*
1 *cucumber, peeled and sliced thin, marinated in juice of*
   1 *lemon for* ½ *hour, and then drained.*

Place whole duck in a pot with 2 cups water and next 6 ingredients. Cover and simmer for 2 hours. Add bamboo shoots and simmer another ½ hour. Skim off and discard all the duck fat you can. Remove duck to platter and garnish with raw scallions, tomato, green pepper, and cucumber. Accompany duck with rice or noodles and some of the mushroom-bamboo-shoot gravy from pot. *Makes 4 servings.*

Latticed Omelets

These shrimp-flavored Siamese omelets have to be made one at a time, but they can be kept in a warming oven. I first ate one of them in Bangkok, where the cooking struck me as a happy marriage of Chinese and Indian, with some original contributions. The fresh fruits in Thailand were especially varied and fine. One day on impulse I bought a new one (new to me) in the street, a large sort of grapefruit called a *durian*. Everybody laughed at me and said I'd better put it out on the terrace of my hotel room because it had a terrible odor. They also said its taste was indescribable—maybe like garlic ice cream. (Maybe they said *rotten* garlic ice cream.) The next day I took it along on a picnic, and people laughed at me again because it is considered to be an aphrodisiac.

½ pound shrimps, shelled, de-veined, and diced
1 small can water chestnuts, drained and diced
1 small hot green chili pepper, seeded and minced
1 tablespoon ground coriander
2 tablespoons patis
½ cup vegetable oil
4 eggs, well beaten
Fresh coriander or parsley, chopped

Combine first 5 ingredients and allow to marinate for 10 minutes or more. Sauté mixture in 2 tablespoons of oil until shrimps turn pink. Cool. In another pan heat remaining oil and dribble in egg by dipping one hand in bowl of beaten eggs and letting the egg fall from the tips of your fingers. Move your hand across the pan in both directions to make a kind of lattice or net, thin, and large enough to allow folding in from each of four sides. Use ¼ of beaten egg. When lattice is cooked, lift out and drain. Put a large pinch of fresh coriander in the center, plus 2 tablespoons of the shrimp mixture, then fold over the sides to make a square. Place in a warming oven and make the rest of the omelets. *Makes 4 servings.*

Chicken Rose Salad

Another exotic dish from Thailand, this salad takes its name not from the fact that you arrange it to look like a rose (you don't) but from one of its ingredients: rose petals. Make sure the roses have not been sprayed.

1 *large onion, chopped*
2 *tablespoons vegetable oil*
10 *cloves garlic, sliced*
3 *cups cooked chicken, shredded*
½ *cup chopped peanuts*

2 *tablespoons* patis
2 *tablespoons* soy sauce
2 *tablespoons lime juice*
2 *tablespoons brown sugar*
Petals of 10 roses from your garden

Fry onion in oil until brown (not golden, but really brown). Add garlic, and continue frying until it turns brown too. Cool. Combine all remaining ingredients except rose petals, and toss well. Mix in rose petals lightly. Garnish with fried onion and garlic. *Makes 4 servings.*

Shreds of Gold

A Chinese woman who lived in Thailand for some years told me this was one of the Thai dishes she had adopted and taken back home to Formosa.

1½ *cups sugar*	12 *egg yolks*
1½ *cups water*	1 *egg white*

To make syrup, boil sugar and water to a temperature of 232° on candy thermometer (until syrup threads). Strain egg yolks through fine sieve, add white, and mix. Using a small funnel or paper cone, make small nests or cubes of egg thread in syrup. When eggs set, lift out with tongs and place on plate to cool. If you keep the syrup very hot, the cubes will be hard when they cool; if you cool the syrup somewhat, they will be chewy. Take your choice. *Makes 8 servings.*

Avocado-Coffee Milkshake

1 *large avocado, mashed*	4 *cups milk*
1 *large cup espresso coffee*	2 *tablespoons sugar*

Mix all ingredients in electric blender, or beat with egg beater until smooth. Pour over crushed ice in tall glasses. Indonesians might add some strings of cold vermicelli, but I don't find this essential. *Makes 6 servings.*

Strawberry Pavlova

Berries, meringue, and whipped cream—many cuisines seem to have a version of this heavenly combination. This one of Australian origin must have been invented for a visit of the famous dancer. It is also sometimes made with passion fruit (a purple sweet-sour fruit native to Australia, as well as South America) and bananas, or with a caramel custard filling.

Buy a 10-inch ring of meringue if you can, or make your own as follows:

6 egg whites   *1½ cups sugar*
¼ teaspoon salt   *1 teaspoon vanilla*
1½ teaspoons cream of
  tartar

Beat egg whites until surface is frothy, sprinkle on salt and cream of tartar, and beat until stiff. Spread a thin layer of mixture on a flat ovenproof plate, or in a 10-inch circle on a cooky

172

sheet. Pile up remaining mixture on top of this layer in a ring, leaving center hollow. Bake at 200° for 1 hour, then turn off oven but leave in meringue—overnight if possible. When ready to use, fill center with sweetened whipped cream, and cover with 1 pint fresh strawberries, lightly crushed. Or leave part of the berries firm and make a sauce by crushing the remaining berries and flavoring with kirsch. *Makes 6 servings.*

Colonial Goose
(Stuffed Lamb)

This delicious stuffed lamb comes from New Zealand, where they have far more sheep than geese. Ask your butcher to bone either a leg or shoulder of lamb, or to order you a leg of mutton if you want to be really colonial about it.

1 large onion, chopped	1 teaspoon thyme
2 tablespoons vegetable oil	1/2 teaspoon sage
1/2 cup melted butter	1 egg, beaten
1 cup diced Smithfield ham	Salt and pepper
1 cup bread crumbs	1 leg of lamb, boned
1/4 cup minced parsley	

To make the stuffing, sauté onion in oil until translucent. Add all remaining ingredients, including salt and pepper to taste, warm and mix well. Place stuffing in center of carefully-boned meat. Wrap and tie meat around stuffing, rub over outside with salt and pepper, and roast on rack in 450° oven for no more than 15 minutes per pound. Carve in thin slices with a sharp knife. Meat should be pink and juicy—even quite rare if your guests will accept it. *A medium-sized leg of lamb should make 6 servings.*

SECTION SIX

The Caribbean Sea

THE CARIBBEAN SEA

Introduction

THE first time I ever ate an avocado was in Spokane, Washington, in the summer of 1939. Recently arrived from Europe, we were spending our summer vacation touring the country, on our way to the fair in San Francisco, stopping to meet my husband's architect-colleagues in each big city. Everyone was exceptionally hospitable, and it was a wonderful trip. We were also introduced to a number of new foods, and certainly the most wonderful was the avocado.

Actually I didn't know what I was getting into. It said "Alligator Pear" on the menu, and obviously I couldn't resist ordering that; but what would it be? I was expecting a pear like other pears, I guess—a sweet fruit, but perhaps with a long hard tail and some sort of a jaw. What came was the beautifully colored, velvety textured, creamy tasting special kind of pear—how can you describe it? It seemed nourishing and filling, and very different from every other fruit. The reason I recall the avocado here is that it is so popular in the Caribbean and in Mexico. I've managed to include four ways of serving it in this section—as a soup, an appetizer, a hot salad, and a dessert.

Peter's friend David Loth who met us once in Haiti to work on *The Book of the Seven Seas* wrote in his Preface to *The Peter Freuchen Reader* that Peter and he spent one hot afternoon on the waterfront at Port-au-Prince trying to find out why there were so many fish in the sea and so few on the market. "He interviewed fishermen, market stall keepers, barefoot women

COOKBOOK of the SEVEN SEAS

shoppers, port officials, members of the United Nations technical mission. Finally he established to his own satisfaction that the problem was lack of ice. In that climate fish spoil in four hours without refrigeration. Ice put the price out of the people's reach, and it was impossible to get the catch from the fishing grounds to the consumer in four hours.

"'I never knew before how lucky the Eskimos are,' Peter commented. 'After all, they have been quick-freezing meat for hundreds of years, and these poor people cannot even keep a fish overnight.'"

I've since been told that the Caribbean waters are "fished out," but whether there's any sense in that observation I don't know. I know I've eaten good fish there, as well as pork and chicken and vegetables and especially good fruits. When Peter and I visited Jamaica we were overwhelmed by the big trays of fruit that came to us every morning—every kind that grows so beautifully in the tropics, particularly mangoes. And we loved drinking fresh coconut milk.

Peter always liked sweet potatoes, which are plentiful in the Caribbean. And we both very much enjoyed the baked bananas flamed with rum or cognac. A day-long operation like roasting a young pig on a spit and basting it carefully with honey and seasonings appealed to us. It gave a double pleasure of anticipation while the feast was being slowly brought to the point of perfection, then enjoyment of it to complete the day. I knew something of the same experience from visits to the market, or merely from watching the women in Haiti walk down the road that led from the mountains, with baskets of colorful fruits and vegetables balanced on their heads.

It was many years later that I visited Puerto Rico. There I was rather surprised to find the manager of the estate where I was a guest reading one of Peter's books about the Arctic. Greenland seemed very remote, and I thought it must be somewhat hard for anyone in the tropics to comprehend. Still, many Puerto Ricans have visited New York and seen cold weather. Finally I was overcome by curiosity, and I asked the manager,

Luis Maldonado, if he had ever been where it was cold. Had he ever seen snow and ice?

"Oh yes," he replied casually, "I was in Thule for two months cooking for the American army."

In addition to a selection of Caribbean recipes, I've reached over to include Mexico here and made a gesture or two toward South America. Peter took a trip around South America in 1935 as a guest of Pan American Airways, but I've never been able to visit there. If I could, I'm sure I'd want to double the size of my book. They say that Peru has two hundred varieties of potatoes. And a great many of corn. And marinated raw fish. Argentinians eat enough beef to make Texans look anemic. I wonder, do all the Danish farmers who settle there give up their smørrebrød for thick steaks? They make good wine in both Chile and Argentina. Brazil is bigger than anywhere else and seems to have some of everything.

Well, it's a very big world to fit into one book, and the job has to be done selectively. I've managed to include two ways of seasoning marinated raw fish. And the only tripe recipe in the book. If you ever eat tripe, this deserves a place with the better-known French and Italian methods of preparation.

Someone asked me just where they grow chestnuts in Latin America. I don't know, but my roast chicken recipe came from down there—maybe the Argentine.

If you've managed the shopping for the earlier sections you won't have any trouble with this one. In case you're just beginning here, hot green peppers, fresh ginger, and fresh coriander are all available in Chinese groceries; the first two can also be found in Puerto Rican groceries, the first and third in Mexican, the first in Italian. Ordinary green tomatoes often turn up in supermarkets, but a different variety from Mexico called *tomatillo* (or a purée made from it) can be bought canned in Spanish groceries. Shallots are sold in some fancy groceries, or you can substitute the white part of scallions. I buy dried chestnuts in an Italian market. Cooking bananas are sold in Puerto Rican groceries.

All avocados have a buttery texture (they're the only fruit with a high fat content) and nutty flavor, but there are different varieties with considerable differences in quality. I like the smooth shiny brighter-green-skinned ones best. Buy them when they are just beginning to soften and keep them at room temperature until they are very soft. Then you can refrigerate them and keep them for several days more.

Chicken Avocado Soup

4 *cups strong chicken broth*   Lemon juice
2 *avocados*   1 *cup clam juice or fish*
Cayenne pepper   bouillon

Heat the seasoned chicken broth and stir in 1 avocado well
mashed. Add cayenne to taste. Cube the other avocado, divide
it between 6 soup plates, and sprinkle with lemon juice. Now
add to the soup 1 cup of clam juice or any stock you may have
from cooking fish, shrimp, or lobster. Or if you want a richer
soup, add 1 cup of cream in place of clam juice. Pour over
cubed avocado in soup plates. *Makes 6 servings.*

Guacamole

Even people who don't generally think much of avocados admit
that this Mexican salad or dip shows them off at their best.
There are many schools of thought on guacamole, some contend-
ing that the avocado should be mashed as smooth as possible,
others that it should be in chunks, some holding that it should
contain tomatoes, others that it should be all green (that still
allows for sour green tomatoes), some feeling that it must be
heavy with pungent Mexican parsley (*cilantro,* or fresh coriander), some prefering onion, some garlic.

2 *avocados, mashed*   2 *small green tomatoes,*
  smooth   *chopped*
1 *hot green chili pepper,*   ¼ *cup chopped* cilantro
  minced   *(fresh coriander)*
1 *clove garlic, minced*   1 *tablespoon lime juice*
                                       Salt

Combine all ingredients, adding salt to taste. Chill. Serve
with tortillas, tostadas, Fritos, or sesame crackers. *Makes 6 appetizer servings.*

181

Flounder Seviche

The marinated raw fish of Mexico and South America can be either plain or fancy, sweet or hot, and the two recipes given here are chosen for contrast. I use flounder and scallops because they are plentiful and good where I live, but you may use any other salt-water fish with white meat such as bass or red snapper, and other raw shellfish.

1 pound flounder fillets
½ cup lemon juice
1 small hot green chili pepper, seeded and minced

2 small onions, sliced thin
Juice of ½ orange
Salt and pepper
2 tablespoons chopped fresh coriander or parsley

Cut fish into small fingers or shreds. Marinate in lemon juice for 2 hours at room temperature or overnight in refrigerator. Drain. Add next three ingredients, plus salt and pepper to taste. Chill. Garnish with fresh coriander or parsley. *Makes 4 appetizer servings.*

Scallop Seviche

1 pound bay scallops, or sea scallops cut in two
½ cup lemon juice
1 large ripe tomato, peeled, seeded, and chopped
1 sweet green pepper chopped
¼ cup cooked corn kernels
2 tablespoons olive oil
1 teaspoon oregano
1 small hot green chili pepper, seeded and minced
Juice of 1 lime
½ teaspoon sugar
Salt and pepper

1 *purple onion, sliced thin*
½ *avocado, cut in thin strips*
2 *tablespoons chopped fresh coriander*

Marinate scallops in lemon juice for 2 hours at room temperature or overnight in refrigerator. Drain. Add next 8 ingredients, plus salt and pepper to taste. If you like hot food, use several chili peppers instead of one. Mix well and chill. Serve garnished with thin onion rings, avocado strips, and coriander. *Makes 4 appetizer servings.*

Pickled Oysters

2 *½-pint containers fresh*
  oysters
2 *teaspoons lemon juice*
½ *teaspoon salt*
¼ *cup olive oil*
2 *cloves garlic, crushed*

6 *peppercorns*
2 *small hot green chili*
  peppers, seeded and cut
  in strips
½ *cup mild vinegar*

Add lemon juice and salt to oysters with their juice and bring to boil. Drain oysters (reserving liquid) and fry in oil until edges curl. Remove and drain. Reduce temperature of oil and fry garlic and peppercorns until garlic colors. Drain. Now combine oyster-lemon juice, fried oysters, garlic, and peppercorns adding green peppers and vinegar. Marinate and chill overnight. *Makes 6 appetizer servings.*

Sautéed Ginger Shrimps

Sautéed slowly in lots of butter, these shrimps come out of the pan as tender and juicy as when they went in.

2 pounds shrimps, shelled and de-veined
6 tablespoons butter
4 shallots, minced

2 teaspoons minced ginger root
2 tablespoons lime juice
Cayenne, salt and pepper

Sauté or stew the shrimps slowly in butter with shallots and ginger. Cooking time will depend on size of shrimps, but stop as soon as they are pink all the way through. Add lime juice, cayenne, salt, and pepper to taste, and heat through. I sometimes add a vegetable, such as okra or squash, that has been cooked separately. *Makes 6 servings.*

Sardine Pie

Peoples of the Caribbean and Latin America enjoy an endless variety of meat-filled fritters, turnovers, pastries, and pies. Most of them are deep-fried, but one of my favorites is this sardine pie, which is baked. Use your favorite pastry recipe or mix to bake a well-done 9-inch pie shell. Then prepare the following filling.

1 pound fresh or canned sardines
1/4 cup vegetable oil
2 large onions, chopped
1/2 cup coarsely chopped parsley
1 cup Italian peeled tomatoes, well drained
Salt and pepper
1 lemon, cut into wedges

If you live where fresh sardines are available, poach them and discard heads and major bones. Or use drained canned sardines, removing backbones. Sauté onion in oil until golden. Add parsley and tomatoes, salt and pepper to taste. Arrange fish in pastry shell and pour sauce over them. Bake in 400° oven for 15 minutes, and serve with lemon wedges. *Makes 4 servings.*

Red Snapper à la Veracruzana

1 3-*pound red snapper*
1 *tablespoon salt*
1 *lemon*
4 *tablespoons vegetable oil*
2 *large onions, sliced*
4 *cloves garlic, sliced*
2 *cups peeled Italian to-matoes with juice*

¼ *cup chopped green olives*
¼ *cup chopped ripe olives*
1 *tablespoon capers*
2 *hot green chili peppers*

Rub fish with salt and juice extracted from lemon. To make sauce, sauté onion in oil until golden, add garlic and continue cooking until it colors. Add tomatoes, olives, capers, and hot peppers (left whole), and mix well. Place fish in this sauce, cover, and simmer until it tests done. Remove to serving platter and cover with sauce. In serving, give one of the whole hot peppers to any fire-eaters among your guests. *Makes 4 servings.*

Loin of Pork San Juan

1 5-pound pork loin roast
1 tablespoon salt
1 teaspoon pepper
¼ cup lard or vegetable oil
2 tablespoons capers
6 cloves garlic
¼ cup chopped ripe olives
¼ cup raisins
2 tablespoons brown sugar
6 medium potatoes, peeled and quartered
Juice of 1 lime

Rub meat with salt and pepper and brown well in fat. Pour off fat, add next 5 ingredients plus 2 cups water. Simmer for 2 hours, turning once or twice. Add potatoes and simmer until they are done, perhaps another hour if the heat is really low. Remove meat and potatoes to serving platter. Skim off all the fat you can, and thicken sauce if necessary with a little flour or cornstarch. Add lime juice and serve with meat. *Makes 6 servings.*

Carbonada

The Flemish *carbonnade* of beef, a stew made with beer, becomes a delicately sweet-and-sour dish (less obvious than the usual Chinese sugar-and-vinegar sweets-and-sours) in Spain and Latin America, where it brings fruits and vegetables together in the same pot with meat. As a party dish, you can give it the following spectacular presentation, in a whole pumpkin.

2 pounds tender beef, cut in small cubes
¼ cup olive oil
2 large onions, chopped
1 large tomato, peeled, seeded, and chopped
3 potatoes, peeled and cubed
2 pears, peeled and sliced
2 peaches, peeled and sliced
4 plums, peeled and sliced
2 tablespoons raisins
1 cup white wine, dry Madeira, or sherry
1 medium pumpkin, top removed and seeded
2 tablespoons butter, melted
Salt and pepper

Brown beef lightly in olive oil. Add onion and cook until translucent. Add next 7 ingredients, cover, and simmer 1 hour. Butter, salt and pepper inside of pumpkin well. Pour in stew, replace top, and bake in 325° oven until pumpkin is tender. Taste and correct seasoning. The sweet-sour taste of Madeira especially suits this dish, but the acid of any wine helps balance the sweetness of the fruits. *Makes 6 servings.*

Mexican Tripe Stew

I hope you can still find canned hominy—it seems to be disappearing from the markets, and it saves a good part of the work that Mexicans put into this excellent way of fixing tripe.

4 pounds tripe	1 tablespoon paprika
1 veal knuckle or other bones	1 teaspoon crushed hot red pepper
4 cloves garlic	2 cups hominy
2 large onions, chopped	2 tablespoons lime juice
1 tablespoon salt	2 teaspoons oregano
1 teaspoon ground cumin	

Cut tripe into small bite-sized strips—the Mexicans sometimes almost mince it. Simmer together with next 7 ingredients plus 6 cups water until tender, up to 12 hours. (Add more water if necessary.) Add hominy, lime juice, and oregano, and heat through. Like so many other Mexican dishes, this can also take a garnish of chopped fresh coriander. *Makes 8 servings.*

Roast Chicken Stuffed with Chestnuts

I use dried chestnuts for convenience, but if you can't get them or prefer fresh ones, buy twice the weight.

1 5-pound roasting chicken	Chicken giblets
2 cloves garlic, sliced	1/2 cup chopped scallions
1/2 cup dry white wine	1/2 cup chopped parsley
1/4 cup lemon juice	1/4 cup melted butter
1/4 pound dried chestnuts	Salt and pepper

Rub chicken inside and out with mixture of garlic, wine, and lemon juice; then marinate in this mixture for 2 hours at room temperature, turning occasionally. If you have remembered to soak the dried chestnuts overnight, now simmer them until tender; but if you forgot to soak them, bring them quickly to a boil, then turn off fire and let them stand in the hot water for 1 hour, then simmer. Drain chestnuts and use the water to cook the giblets. Drain (reserve liquid) and chop giblets, and add to chestnuts, which you have broken into 2 or more pieces each. Add all remaining ingredients, salt and pepper to taste. Add as much of liquid in which giblets were cooked as mixture will absorb without becoming soupy. Stuff and sew up chicken. Roast breast side down in a covered pan at 325° for 1 hour and 20 minutes. Then roast breast side up, uncovered, for 1 hour more, basting every 15 minutes with marinade and any remaining giblet liquid. *Makes 4 servings.*

Stewed Fresh Ham with Bananas

Green cooking bananas are a source of starch, and if you can't get them substitute sweet potatoes or yams. Don't use ripe bananas, whose starch has turned into sugar.

½ fresh ham (about 4 pounds)
2 tablespoons olive oil
1 teaspoon pepper
1 tablespoon salt
6 cloves garlic
2 bay leaves

1 large onion, chopped
1 cup white wine
3 large cooking bananas, quartered (available at Puerto Rican groceries)
Juice of 1 lime

Remove any skin and excess fat from fresh ham, then brown it in oil. Add next 6 ingredients, plus 4 cups water, cover, and simmer for 2 hours. Add bananas and cook until tender. Sprinkle with lime juice. *Makes 6 servings.*

Potatoes with Cold Cheese Sauce

I like the contrast between hot potatoes and cold sauce. Or you can have the potatoes cold too, and end up with a kind of potato salad.

6 medium potatoes, baked or boiled in jackets
1 cup cottage cheese
4 yolks of hardboiled eggs

1 hot green chili pepper, seeded and minced
¼ cup olive oil
Salt

Cook potatoes either way to eat hot, or boil and peel them if you plan to eat them cold. To make sauce put cottage cheese and egg yolks through a sieve, mix in chili pepper (or several peppers, to taste), and dribble in olive oil while working mixture with a wooden spoon. Add salt to taste. Cut open tops of hot potatoes or slice cold ones and spoon on sauce. *Makes 6 servings.*

Winter Squash

Summer squashes seem to me at their best steamed or boiled whole (cooked the minimum time), then cubed or sliced and eaten unpeeled with a touch of butter. Winter squashes benefit from a bit more manipulation. This recipe from South America makes a rich dish good to serve with plain broiled meat or fish.

1 pound butternut or any winter squash, peeled and cubed

¾ cup yellow cornmeal

¼ cup milk

2 tablespoons butter

¼ pound cheddar cheese, shredded

Cook squash in boiling salted water until tender. Drain and mash. Add cornmeal, milk, and butter; cook and stir for 10 minutes on low heat. Then add cheese a little at a time, cooking and stirring another 10 minutes. When well blended, cover and let stand for 10 minutes. *Makes 4 servings.*

Hot Avocado Salad

This reminds me of hot German potato salad, and I make it when I have avocados that are not quite fully ripe.

2 tablespoons oil or bacon fat

1 medium onion, chopped fine

1 large sweet green pepper, chopped fine

½ small hot green chili pepper, seeded and minced

2 large avocados, chopped

¼ cup mild vinegar

¼ pound bacon, fried crisp and crumbled

Fry onion and both peppers in fat until golden. Add avocados and vinegar, toss and heat through. Sprinkle on bacon. No salt or pepper should be needed, but you may add them to taste. *Makes 4 servings.*

Baked Bananas with Honey and Rum

¼ cup butter
6 ripe bananas
6 tablespoons honey

2 tablespoons lemon juice
½ cup rum

Melt butter in baking dish. Peel bananas, cut them in half lengthwise, and place in butter. Mix honey and lemon juice and pour over bananas. Bake at 400° for 15 minutes. Add rum and ignite. This dessert can also be made in a chafing dish, in which case the bananas are cooked in the butter until lightly browned before the honey is added. *Makes 6 servings.*

Sweet Potatoes and Pineapple

This is a dessert from Puerto Rico, and I think it shows a better understanding of sweet potatoes than most of us have. I enjoy sweet potatoes baked in their jackets like Idaho potatoes (or baked and a little bit charred in the cinders of an outdoor fire), served with coarse salt. But when you glaze them, candy them, melt marshmallows on them, etc., I feel you disqualify them for the meat-and-vegetable course. Many Latin Americans face this issue squarely by turning them into a dessert: sweet potatoes and pumpkin, sweet potatoes and bananas—and in this case, a combination of sweet potatoes and pineapple that almost makes a candy.

1 pound boiled sweet potatoes, peeled and mashed
1 cup crushed pineapple with juice

½ cup sugar
2 egg yolks, beaten
¼ cup slivered almonds

Put potatoes through a sieve and mix with pineapple and sugar. If you use fresh pineapple, you may wish to add more sugar. Now cook on low fire, stirring constantly, for about 20 minutes or until quite thick. Stir in beaten egg a little at a time and cook 5 minutes more. Spread on greased plate, sprinkle with almonds, and cut into diamond shapes when cold. Serve with strong coffee at the end of dinner or in mid-afternoon. *Makes 6 servings.*

Avocado Whip

This rich and extraordinary fruit has become very popular in salads and appetizers. Like other types of pears, it also makes a good dessert.

2 large ripe avocados   *2 tablespoons lime juice*
½ cup confectioners' sugar

Cut avocados in half lengthwise and remove pulp carefully, keeping skins intact. Mash pulp until smooth, beating in sugar and lime juice. Spoon mixture back into skins and chill. *Makes 4 servings.*

Angostura Grapefruit

If it sometimes seems like you won't ever find another use for that bottle of bitters you got for making occasional Old Fashioneds, this will help you along. Since both grapefruit and Angostura originate in the West Indies, the marriage is especially compatible.

2 large grapefruits   Angostura bitters
4 heaping teaspoons brown
  sugar

Cut each grapefruit in half, remove any seeds, loosen sections, sprinkle on sugar, and add about 10 drops of Angostura bitters to each half. Allow to marinate for 10 minutes before serving. *Makes 4 servings.*

SECTION SEVEN

The Sea Around Us

THE SEA AROUND US

Introduction

THE first summer Peter and I were married we took a house on Fire Island. Our life there was simple, if not primitive, and we enjoyed simple pleasures like sitting on the boardwalk eating watermelon and spitting the seeds into the poison ivy. I had heard so much about Peter's island in Denmark, Enehoje, where he settled and took up farming in the late 1930's, that I wanted to show him the island frequented by many of my artist friends. Peter called Fire Island "a delightful place," and we made many friends there whom we went back to visit in later years. One of them told us later that she couldn't imagine what kind of strange animal had set foot on the beach when she first saw the alternating single footprint and hole made where Peter walked with his stump.

The following year we found a house in Noank, Connecticut, an old sailing town that suited us perfectly; and thereafter we divided our time between Noank and our New York City apartment, except for Peter's lecture tours and other travels. When we bought the house in Noank the kitchen had to be remodeled. It was ideally situated for anyone who likes to live in the kitchen, with two exposures overlooking Fishers Island Sound. Everything was installed to our own design, with walls and rubber-tile floor in light blue, appliances and cabinets in white, and china of a blue-and-white pattern from Finland. There was just enough room to put in a breakfast table.

Right outside the kitchen was a large terrace, a nice cool

place to serve supper. We built a barbecue pit not far away, near the water, and used it when there was not too much breeze. Water came from our own well, pure enough to drink, but actually we preferred drinking water from a spring in the nearby woods. We fetched the spring water ourselves, filling several gallon bottles at a time. We liked to do things ourselves, whenever we could, instead of hiring someone to do them. We filled up holes in our driveway with clam shells. To keep the grass under control, we decided to raise a few sheep, putting up the fences ourselves, at considerable pain. There was a small uninhabited island nearby which Peter thought was an idyllic place to swim except that it was covered with poison ivy. He talked about buying it one day and putting the sheep there to eat up the ivy. But unfortunately some neighborhood dogs jumped over our fences and killed our three sheep, Hannibal, the father, Kulabak, the mother, and the darling baby lamb, Jackson. It was a terrible loss. (We'd started out with Hannibal alone, but he was very dull-spirited and unhappy until we got Kulabak. It must have been love at first sight, for when she arrived I actually saw his face light up.) I didn't want any more sheep, so we bought a lawnmower.

In the garden at Noank we grew parsley, chives, dill, and tarragon. We had gooseberry bushes, and among the vegetables were tomatoes, leeks, and corn—with his sweet tooth, Peter loved corn, and he frequently sent cans of it to relatives and friends in Denmark—and always lots of asparagus. American asparagus matures in less time than the asparagus in Europe, where it is covered and nursed along for three years to obtain those giant white stalks. Peter remembered hearing that when his family had bought a house in Denmark his mother decided not to plant asparagus in the garden because it took so long to mature. By the time we were growing it every year in Noank the property had been in his family about eighty-five years, but still nobody wanted to risk planting asparagus and not being there to enjoy it.

We also grew one plant that Peter detested—rhubarb. I like it, but it was much too sour for him, and whenever he saw me cooking it he made terrible faces and tried to persuade me to put in bicarbonate of soda to neutralize the acid.

Another vegetable he didn't care much about was eggplant. But he loved onions, putting them with lots of other foods in simple home cooking. When I was working in town or away traveling he frequently made himself a large pot of onion-rich Sailors' Stew (the recipe given in Section 1) and reheated it in a double boiler a portion at a time. Peter was a capable cook, although he didn't bother much about exact recipes.

One of our most popular dinners in Noank was plain boiled lobsters with drawn butter. We bought the live lobsters right next door, so close to our house that I usually started heating the water in the lobster pot before I went down to get them, then dropped them right in when I came back. Living there in a fishing port, we could often buy lobsters that had lost one of their claws—called culls—for much less money than the perfect ones, because the culls couldn't be sold to restaurants. We nearly always ate our lobsters outdoors on the terrace, equipped with nutcrackers and special lobster forks and bright red hand towels in place of napkins.

We had many guests in Noank (also in New York), and sometimes we observed the old custom of passing along the job of fixing meals to anyone who criticized the food. But there was never a problem of doing dishes because Peter didn't mind doing them himself. In fact he said it was relaxing, like chopping wood. He just pulled up a kitchen chair, sat down, and sang old Danish folk songs as he washed away. He knew a lot of songs, mostly about sailors and their sweethearts. He claimed that he had scared the wolves away with his singing when he lived alone in the Arctic.

Once when I was away and Peter entertained some visitors he wrote me, "I find that you and I live very simply compared to what others think they have got to have." One of his menus at that time was broiled swordfish with parsley butter, carrots, green beans, melon with blueberries, and Greenland Coffee. Another menu, for an informal snowballing party of fourteen, was *fricadeller* (meatballs—Peter had tried to get a young shark but had no luck), red cabbage, mashed potatoes, cherries and boysenberries with ice cream, and Greenland Coffee. Once he wrote that he had got a nice duck and some chestnuts which he toasted in salt, another time six fresh herrings, which he fried.

Whenever I happened to be away, Peter ate very simply at home, often lunching on fruit and milk, and fixing fresh eels or a casserole of rice and mock turtle stew (a canned specialty from Denmark) for dinner. But he was frequently invited out, and often he pitched in to help with the preparation. Once there was a whole bushel of crabs, about 180 of them, which he cooked, while the hosts were making clam chowder. He reported this feast to me while I was staying in Paris for *Vogue* to sketch the new collection. The magazine put me up at the Crillon, and as I was usually too busy to go down for regular meals I had room service send up some of the appetizing cold foods the French do to perfection: poached chicken with the finest mayonnaise, little filled rolls of the most delicate ham, and eggs in aspic with truffles and slices of tongue. I believe my interest in aspics began at this time, and it has never waned.

Back in New York, I went on sketching, and often had fashion models coming to the apartment for work. These girls had a real diet problem, for if they didn't stay thin (and that meant really gaunt) they wouldn't get work. Whenever I saw one of them looking as if she might be about to faint, I'd ask what she'd had for breakfast. The answer was usually either black coffee or Coca-Cola, or sometimes nothing. As soon as I heard this I'd get out the crackers and cheese and milk, and in a few minutes we'd be able to go on.

In New York we also dined out a lot, and we couldn't resist either the fascinating restaurants or unusual international parties. Peter wrote regularly for his Danish newspaper about the debates at the United Nations. "Even if the many speeches and endless meetings have not always seemed very constructive," he noted, "I have found the contact with people from every nation and every race most inspiring." Because he was so fond of sweets, one of the places Peter liked to go in New York was Robert Day-Dean's, a mid-town caterer's with a window display of cakes and pastries. He called it "the immoral place." He was also very fond of every kind of pancakes and waffles, and loved every variation from crepes suzette to plain flapjacks with maple syrup. He also liked to make and flip them himself, though he

learned they weren't the best thing for his diet. "I have been invited to have pancakes today, so I won't eat anything before," he wrote once. And again, "I went down this morning to eat breakfast and was going to order eggs. But suddenly the devil took over my soul and I ordered griddlecakes. I regretted it immediately when I had said it. But it was too late."

On his lecture tours Peter discovered many regional American specialities, such as Oysters Rockefeller in New Orleans, and I have given recipes for a few of the more unusual ones. He liked to bring home new ideas all the time, and so do I. At the same time, there were some traditional practices that he observed all his life. Every morning when he opened the door of the refrigerator the first thing he did was to turn over the container of eggs. It was to "give the eggs some exercise" and keep the yolks in the middle. If I had gone into the kitchen ahead of him he always asked, "Did you turn the eggs?" I got in the habit, and I still do it.

Each year I keep learning new things about food, and my cooking changes in various ways. I've just recently remarried, and we've done a lot of entertaining, bringing together my old friends and my husband's friends and family. My husband, Henry Gale, is a New York lawyer and a gourmet who buys the best wines and travels in France with the *Guide Michelin* in hand. Our many recent guests have given me the opportunity to re-test the recipes for this book, which might therefore be appropriately dedicated to him and to them. Whatever direction our culinary path takes in the future, I doubt that it will stray very far from the rewarding bounty of the seven seas.

Kippered Herring Pâté

You can buy cans of kippers in every supermarket. Besides eating them broiled or sautéed (really just heated through), with or without scrambled eggs, for breakfast or lunch, and in a souffllé, you can make a good fish-paste out of them to use as a first course at dinner or in Danish open-faced sandwiches. I invented this recipe for a friend who loves liver pâté but had to give it up when his doctor put him on a low-cholesterol diet.

1 12-ounce can kippered herring (plain, not in tomato sauce)
6 thin slices bread, crusts trimmed off
½ cup Madeira

2 cloves garlic, finely minced
¼ cup lemon juice
¼ cup corn oil
Salt and pepper

Remove bones from herrings. Leave skin or remove it, as you like. Break up bread and soak in Madeira. Combine all ingredients and mash or beat until well mixed and smooth. Pack into small bowl or crock, cover, and chill thoroughly. Serve with bread, scallions, or spears of seeded cucumber. *If divided into 8 servings, each will be just over 200 calories* (exclusive of accompanying bread—scallions and cucumbers go free).

Green Peppers and Anchovies

The Italians have a delicious appetizer of roast peppers and anchovies—loaded with olive oil. My low-calorie American version is good and easy—no cooking.

1 large green pepper
1 2-ounce can flat fillets of anchovies

Seed pepper and cut carefully lengthwise in narrow strips, about ⅜″ wide (to fit width of anchovy fillet). Drain anchovies of oil and place one on each piece of pepper. For color contrast, you can use both green and red (sweet) peppers. *Makes about 20 strips.*

Poached Fish Livers

If your local fish market sells whole fresh codfish or striped bass, ask the fish merchant to save you the livers. They are inexpensive, healthy, and delicate in taste when carefully prepared.

1 pound fish livers
1 teaspoon salt
5 peppercorns

2 bay leaves
Lemon juice
Salt and pepper

Cover livers with water, add salt, peppercorns, and bay leaves, bring to boil, and simmer for 15 minutes. Drain and let cool. Purée in blender or put through sieve, chill in refrigerator, and mix in lemon juice, salt, and pepper to taste. Serve with hot buttered toast and thin slices of lemon, or stuffed into hollowed-out cherry tomatoes. Or use as a dressing for fish. Eat fish livers the day you prepare them because they are likely to turn bitter if kept overnight. *Makes 8 appetizer servings.*

She-Crab Soup

Carolina she-crab soup is a kind of oyster stew made with crab meat and slightly thickened with cracker crumbs. It isn't too creamy to overwhelm the delicate taste of fresh crab. I think the soup gets its name because you make a point of adding any roe you find with the crab meat.

1 *pound container fresh crab meat, or meat and roe picked from fresh steamed crabs*
4 *tablespoons butter*
1 *pint milk*
1 *pint cream*
4 *tablespoons fine cracker crumbs*
Dash of mace
Salt and pepper
4 *tablespoons Madeira or whiskey*
Minced parsley

Pick over the crab meat carefully, removing all bits of cartilage and shell. The job will be easier if you use lump crab meat rather than flake or regular, but the taste is the same. Claw meat, which is darker in color, and lower in price, has a nice nutty flavor. Sauté crab in butter until warmed through. Add milk and heat until just below boiling. Add cream and cracker crumbs, stirring and heating slowly. Do not allow to boil. When good and hot, stir in mace, salt, and pepper to taste. Put 1 tablespoon of Madeira in each of four bowls and add soup. Or use whiskey for a sharper taste. Sprinkle with parsley. *Makes 4 servings.*

Clam Chowder

I try to remember that not everybody is as lucky as I am in living where there is always lots of fresh fish in the market. If you make this soup with fresh clams, it's a good idea to grind them for tenderness—that way you run no risk of tough rubbery bits that practically break your teeth, as in so many restaurant chowders. But you can just as well use canned minced clams, which will probably be littlenecks if you live in the East and razor clams in the West.

4 slices bacon, diced
2 small onions, chopped
2 medium potatoes, boiled, peeled, and diced
1 cup clam juice (may be bottled)

Salt and pepper
1 cup minced clams (may be canned)
1 cup cream
Chopped chives

Fry the bacon until very crisp, remove and drain. Fry onion in bacon fat until lightly browned. Combine onions, potatoes, and clam juice. Add any water you may have left from boiling potatoes (there shouldn't be much) and any liquor from minced clams. Salt and pepper to taste and bring to boil. Add minced clams and cream, and heat through but do not boil. Serve garnished with crisp bacon and chives. *Makes 2 servings.* For variation add ½ cup young tender kernels of corn, cut from the cob when in season, or from a can of white shoepeg corn.

Shrimp Gumbo

Gumbos well-thickened with mucilaginous okra or file (sassafras powder) and served on a mound of boiled rice seem to me the Creole equivalent of gummy Chinese-American chop suey. However, this needn't be the case. Everyone agrees that a gumbo has to contain okra, but not all that much. Otherwise, it can accommodate almost any fish or fowl, meat or vegetable you want—whatever you happen to have, or what's cheap. I've had a good gumbo made with nothing more than some chicken stock and leftover meat, onions fried in bacon fat, okra, tomatoes, and sweet potatoes. I suggest shrimp in the following recipe because its flavor is strong enough to stand up well, and because it is available fresh or frozen everywhere. But please substitute crab (also available everywhere frozen and canned) or oysters or anything you prefer.

1/4 cup butter
1 large onion, chopped
2 tablespoons flour
1 large can (2 1/2 cups) Italian peeled tomatoes
1/2 teaspoon Tabasco sauce, or less to taste
2 teaspoons salt
2 bay leaves
3 cups fish or chicken stock
1/2 pound Smithfield ham, diced
1 pound small shrimps, peeled and de-veined
1 package frozen okra, thawed

Sauté onion in butter until golden. Sprinkle on flour and mix well. Add next 5 ingredients, bring to boil, cover and cook on low heat for 10 minutes. Add all remaining ingredients (each pod of okra sliced in 1/2" rounds) and cook another 10 minutes. This produces a soup rather than a thick stew, and I prefer serving it with toasted garlic bread rather than rice. *Makes 4 servings.*

Thick Oyster Stew

As with many other fine foods, the less you do to oysters, the better the results, and the classic oyster stew needs only butter, milk or cream, salt and pepper—no celery, onion, Worcestershire sauce, flour, etc. However, *this* stew is thick with oysters, not with flour, and the result really is a dish of stewed oysters, not a milk soup. The original recipe is said to come from William Paca, one of Maryland's signers of the Declaration of Independence.

½ gallon oysters with liquor	Salt and pepper
½ pound butter	Mace
Flour	½ pint cream

Stew oysters (½ gallon is 8 of the ½ pint containers in which they're usually sold) in their own liquor for 2 minutes. Add butter and continue stewing until edges curl. Add a very light sprinkle of flour to thicken, salt and pepper to taste, and a generous pinch of mace. Add cream just before taking off the fire. *Makes 8 servings.*

Simple Clam Bake

Half the fun of a clam bake is everybody pitching in, fixing and eating everything outdoors, preferably at the shore. Use whatever facilities exist for baking or steaming, and choose any seafood you like that's fresh and plentiful. The greater the amount of food and more elaborate the preparation, the more everyone will probably enjoy it. In case you have to do the job all by yourself, here is a simple way of packaging a clambake for individual service and cooking it on any sort of outdoor grill, instead of spending all day digging a pit. The first part of the preparation can be done at home if you want to save the trouble of taking pots to the shore.

4 dozen soft shell clams	*8 live blue crabs*
12 small white onions	*2 lemons, cut into wedges*
4 small baking potatoes	*Melted butter*
4 ears corn on the cob with husks	

Scrub clams and soak them in sea water or in fresh water with ½ cup salt to 1½ gallons for 1 hour, changing water 3 times. Clams will discharge sand. Parboil onions and potatoes for 15 minutes. Peel back corn husks, remove silk, and replace husks. Wash crabs. Now cut large squares of cheesecloth and aluminum foil, at least 1½' by 3'. In a double layer of cheesecloth place 12 clams, 2 crabs, 3 onions, and 1 each of potatoes and corn. Tie corners of cheesecloth together and place package on a double layer of foil. Pour on 1 cup hot water, fold over foil, and seal edges. Place foil packages on grill 4" from hot coals and leave for 15 minutes on each side. Open 1 package carefully to see if all foods are cooked; nothing in the package needs very long, but heat of coals can vary considerably. Give each guest several lemon wedges and a cup of melted butter. To eat the crabs, first break off the claws, pull off the apron and top shell, and break off the legs. Remove gills and organs in center of body. Slice away top of one side of inner skeleton with small knife and pick out all bits of meat. Repeat on other side. Break shell of each claw and pull out tendons; if meat fails to come out with them, pry it out with the knife. You may want pepper for the potatoes and corn. I like to drink cold beer or white wine with this food. *Makes 4 servings.*

Cioppino

Here is California's gift to the repertory of great fish stews of the world. Nobody seems quite sure of its origin, but probably it was invented by Portuguese fishermen who simply made use of all the most unusual bits of the day's catch. It's traditionally made with red wine, and since California has a red wine of equally uncertain origin, Zinfandel, that's a good one to use both in the pot and the glass. Make it with as few or many fish as you like; I suggest here some that are available almost everywhere.

> 1 *pound shrimps in shells*
> 1 *live lobster or large crab, or 2 frozen rock lobster tails*
> 1 *quart clams or mussels in shells, or a large can of steamed clams, frozen oysters—any mollusks you can find*
> 2 *pounds fresh fish such as bass, or 1 pound frozen fish steaks*
> 2 *ounces dried mushrooms*
> 1/4 *cup olive oil*
> 1 *large onion, chopped*
> 1 *green pepper, chopped*
> 2 *cloves garlic, chopped*
> 1 *large can (2½ cups) Italian peeled tomatoes*
> 2 *cups Zinfandel, or other dry red wine*
> 1/4 *teaspoon dried basil*
> 1/2 *teaspoon dried oregano*
> *Salt and pepper*
> 1/4 *cup minced parsley*

Cut shrimp shells down the back and remove sand vein, but leave shrimps in shells. Cut lobsters in sections, shell and all. Steam mollusks and throw away empty halves of shells. Save water. Cut fish in large bite-sized or serving pieces. Wash mushrooms well and put to soak in warm water. If dried mushrooms are large, they may need to be cut into strips and stems removed. Their flavor is important, but they tend to remain tough practically forever. In large casserole sauté onion and pepper in oil until translucent; add garlic and sauté until it colors. Add tomatoes with their juice, wine, basil, mushrooms with their water, and water from steamed mollusks. If this does not make at least 2 additional cups of liquid, add that much of any fish or chicken stock, or tomato juice. Simmer 15 minutes to marry flavors. Now add shrimps, lobster, and fish to casserole, cover, and cook on a low fire for 10 minutes. Test to see if fish is done, and if it is, add the oregano, salt and pepper to taste, and the mollusks in shells. Cover again and heat for 3 minutes. Like bouillabaisse, this is a dish that cooks quickly once you get all the parts assembled. Serve in large soup plates, well sprinkled with parsley, and with an empty plate at the side for shells. *Makes 6 servings.*

Clam Pie

A New England clam pie can be nothing more than ground fresh clams, seasoned, baked between two layers of pastry. But eastern Long Island seems to make a specialty of this dish, and there everybody does it a different way. At The Springs, East-hampton, where I sometimes spend Labor Day weekend, there's a Clam Pie Festival every year. Both professional chefs and ama-teurs participate, and hundreds of clam pies are made, consumed, or put into freezers. Everyone uses fresh clams, but you can sub-stitute canned clams for convenience.

1 *pound minced or ground raw clams (weight with juice), or 2 8-ounce cans minced clams*
5 *tablespoons butter*
3 *tablespoons flour*
½ *cup cream*
½ *cup clam juice*
2 *tablespoons Madeira or sherry*

1 *medium onion, chopped fine*
1 *small green pepper, chopped*
1 *medium raw potato, diced fine*
½ *teaspoon black pepper*
2 *tablespoons chopped parsley*
½ *recipe rich pie crust*

Drain clams and reserve ½ cup of juice to use in making sauce. Make sauce of 3 tablespoons of the butter, flour, cream, and clam juice, and simmer for 10 minutes. Add Madeira. Sauté onion, green pepper, and potato lightly in remaining butter. Add black pepper and parsley. Combine sautéed vegetables and white sauce, add clams, and pour into lightly greased pie plate. Cover top with crust about ¼″ thick and bake at 400° for 25 minutes, or until golden brown. *Makes 6 servings.*

Poached Striped Bass Béarnaise

Béarnaise sauce is fine for special occasions. The Danes eat it much more frequently than Americans do, and every Danish grocery carries bottled "béarnaise essence," which is a mixture of boiled-down wine, vinegar, and herbs. Peter and I used to serve Whale Steak Béarnaise, and some of my friends still reminisce about it.

2 cups white wine
1 onion, sliced
1 carrot, sliced
½ lemon, sliced
2 sprigs parsley

10 peppercorns
1 tablespoon salt
½ teaspoon thyme
1 bay leaf
1 6-pound striped bass

Combine all ingredients except bass in fish boiler, add 2 cups water, bring to boil, and simmer 15 minutes. Let cool. Lower fish into liquid, add more water if necessary to cover, bring to boil, and simmer 12 to 15 minutes. Lift out carefully, drain, and serve in platter lined with napkin. Make béarnaise according to any standard French cookbook, and serve separately in sauceboat. *Makes 8 servings.*

Baked Connecticut River Shad

We bought the local river shad as often as we could at the fish market near Noank each spring—the season is so short and the shad so delicious. In fact it seemed more delicious there than any shad I have tasted anywhere else.

3 pounds boned shad	*1 tablespoon butter*
¼ teaspoon salt	*½ cup milk*
Pinch of pepper	

Put shad into well-buttered baking dish skin side down. (Each time I do this I'm reminded of putting a pleated silk skirt into a suitcase.) Add salt and pepper, and dot with butter. Bake in 400° oven for 15 minutes. Add milk and bake another 15 minutes, basting occasionally. *Makes 6 servings.*

Baked Bluefish

1 4- to 5-pound bluefish,	*1 tablespoon chopped*
split	*parsley*
Butter	*1 tablespoon lemon juice*
Salt and pepper	*½ cup dry vermouth*
1 large sprig fresh dill, or	
½ teaspoon dried dill-	
weed	

Dot the inside of the fish with butter, sprinkle with salt and pepper, add dill and parsley, and fold halves of fish together. Place fish on its side in shallow buttered baking dish, add lemon

THE SEA AROUND US

juice and vermouth, sprinkle with salt and pepper, and dot top
with butter. Bake uncovered at 425° for 20 to 25 minutes, or
until fish tests done. If you want to make a pretty arrangement
of the fish on a platter, line the baking dish with foil. This helps
you slide the fish out without breaking it. *Makes 6 servings.*

Flounder and Spinach Soufflé

This is a convenient first course for a small dinner party. You
can do all of the work on it before your guests arrive, only finish-
ing it in the oven as they are having their last drink.

3 *medium-sized filets of
flounder*
1 *cup white wine or dry
vermouth*
½ *cup mayonnaise*

1 *package frozen chopped
spinach, cooked and
drained*
Salt and pepper
2 *tablespoons grated Parmesan cheese*
4 *egg whites*

Cut each fish filet in half lengthwise, roll up the 6 pieces,
and secure each one with a toothpick. Place in pan with wine and
poach for 6 minutes. Place in large buttered clam shells or rame-
kins, and remove toothpicks. Mix together mayonnaise, spinach,
salt and pepper to taste, and cheese. Beat egg whites until stiff
and fold into mixture. Spread over fish and bake at 400° for
10 minutes. *Makes 6 servings.*

215

Swordfish Pepper Steak

This is the delicious French pan-broiled *steak au poivre* (not the Chinese sliced beefsteak with green peppers), but made with swordfish instead of beef. You can do it equally well with fresh tuna, and with whale steak, if you live where you can get it. Whale is popular in Japan, and during the Second World War a good deal of it was eaten in England, but today its availability in the western world seems limited to the Eskimos.

> *4 individual swordfish steaks, about* 1/2 *pound each*
> *Flour*
> *2 teaspoons crushed or cracked peppercorns, or less to taste*
> *2 tablespoons butter*
> *Salt*
> *1/4 cup cognac*

Dry the fish, dust with flour, and press the pepper into both sides of each steak. Let stand for 1/2 hour. Heat butter and sauté steaks until brown on both sides. Remove to hot platter and salt to taste. Add cognac to pan, swirl, and scrape, but do not boil. Pour quickly over fish and ignite. *Makes 4 servings.*

Broiled Fresh Tuna with Rosemary

Everybody likes canned tuna fish, but why do so few people eat it fresh? Besides enjoying it raw, like the Japanese, I cook tuna steaks in either of two ways; both require marinating and both have a strong herb flavor.

4 individual tuna steaks,
    about ½ pound each
1 teaspoon dried rosemary,
    crumbled
2 tablespoons lemon juice
¼ cup olive oil

Salt and pepper
4 tablespoons melter but-
    ter
4 tablespoons minced
    parsley

Marinate the fish for 1 hour at room temperature in the rosemary, lemon juice, and oil. Broil (over charcoal if possible) for 3 to 5 minutes on each side, depending on thickness of steaks and distance from fire. Do not overcook. Baste during broiling with any of the marinade that remains (there won't be much). Salt and pepper to taste, and serve with combined butter and parsley. *Makes 4 servings.*

Sautéed Tuna with Tarragon

4 fresh tuna steaks, about ½ pound each
1 tablespoon dried tarragon, crushed
1 cup dry white wine
¼ cup butter
Flour
Salt and pepper

Marinate fish for 1 hour at room temperature in tarragon and wine. Drain and reserve liquid. Heat butter, flour fish lightly, and sauté until done on both sides. Remove from pan to hot platter, salt and pepper to taste. Add marinade to pan, deglaze, and cook on high fire until liquid is reduced. Pour over fish. *Makes 4 servings.*

Baked Cod with Anchovies

Use either a baby cod (also called scrod), a center cut of a larger fish, or frozen cod steaks. (Other frozen fish steaks such as haddock will also do.) This is one of those unusual fish dishes prepared with red wine, so you might like to accompany the fish with a glass of the same.

> 1 2-pound scrod, or 1 pound of codfish steaks
> 1 2-ounce can flat fillets of anchovies
> 1 cup dry red wine
> Pepper

Place 3 or 4 of the anchovies diagonally across the top side of the fish and the rest of the can inside the cavity. Or if you use steaks, make a lattice of anchovies on top. Dribble the oil from the anchovy can over the fish, in an ovenproof dish, and add the wine. Bake at 450° for ½ hour, or until fish tests done, basting every 5 minutes with wine. Pepper well just before serving. You won't need any salt because of the anchovies. *Makes 2 servings.*

Salmon Baked in Sour Cream

Ah, salmon! Perhaps the best ways to eat this noble fish are raw or smoked, cut in thin slices, seasoned with lemon juice and black pepper. Just add good bread and sweet butter. Smoked salmon is also a favorite in Danish open-faced sandwiches. Also high in my affections comes fresh salmon, delicately poached—no more than 8 minutes a pound—so that it stays soft and moist. Eat this either hot with lemon butter or tepid (not really cold) with homemade mayonnaise. Then if you want something a bit fancier, something you can prepare with frozen salmon steaks if you're unable to get fresh salmon, try this recipe.

3 pounds salmon
Salt and pepper
1 tablespoon lemon juice
2 cups sour cream
Any or all of the following:
  1 tablespoon chopped dill
  1 tablespoon chopped chives
  2 tablespoons chopped parsley

Salt and pepper a piece of salmon or salmon steaks lightly and place in greased baking dish. Mix together remaining ingredients and spread over salmon. Bake in 375° oven for ½ hour or until salmon tests done. *Makes 6 servings.*

Salmon Steaks with Caviar Sauce

So many people like plain broiled salmon steaks that maybe I ought to leave well enough alone. My introduction to the crisp surface and special flavor that result from charcoal broiling of salmon came in Portland, Oregon, a lovely city full of flowers, where I stopped on the same 1939 trip that took me to Spokane and San Francisco. In any case, here is something different, if you want a rich and elegant sauce to serve with salmon steaks.

6 *individual-serving salmon steaks*	1½ *cups milk*
Pepper	2 *egg yolks, beaten*
Olive oil	1 *teaspoon lemon juice*
¼ *cup butter*	2 *ounces caviar*
¼ *cup flour*	*Parsley*
	2 *lemons, cut into wedges*

If fresh salmon is unavailable, use frozen steaks. Thaw them out, rub well with pepper and oil, and broil over charcoal (or in hot gas broiler) about 4 minutes on each side, or until they test done. Brush with oil when you turn them over. Make a white sauce of butter, flour, and milk, stir in egg yolks and lemon juice. Stir in caviar carefully, and correct seasoning. Use fresh salmon roe if you are lucky enough to find it, otherwise red caviar out of a jar. Spread sauce over steaks on platter. Garnish with parsley and lemon wedges. *Makes 6 servings*.

Trout with Almonds

Trout ought to travel in a straight line from the mountain brook to the pan of sizzling butter or the pot of vinegar-water—so the experts say, and I'm sure they're right. But if you don't fish, and don't live near a restaurant that keeps trout alive in a tank, do you have to forego this delicacy altogether? Not in my opinion. The taste of almonds enhances the flavor of trout so nicely that you can even do this dish successfully with frozen trout. The trout may come from Denmark, like me, but I like them cooked in an American style, with cornmeal.

4 rainbow trout, or 8 if they are under ½ pound each
Salt and pepper
Yellow cornmeal

6 tablespoons butter
¼ pound sliced almonds
2 tablespoons chopped parsley

Thaw fish if frozen, sprinkle inside and out with salt and pepper, and roll in cornmeal. Fry in butter on a medium fire, turning only once but shaking and basting to keep from sticking. As soon as fish test done, remove to hot platter. Add almonds to butter remaining in pan and cook until golden. Pour over fish and garnish with parsley. *Makes 4 servings.* This makes a dry dish, low in calories. Use more butter if you want it richer.

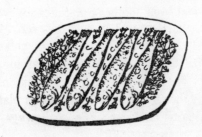

Broiled Mackerel with Mustard

Do people tend to overlook this rich and delicious fish just because it's so cheap? I'm told there are more than twenty species of mackerel, and I'm sure I'd like them all. The commonest two in the market are Spanish mackerel (everywhere) and Boston mackerel (long and thin, east coast only).

> *2 tablespoons melted butter*
> *1 tablespoon mustard, mild or hot according to taste*
> *2 tablespoons lemon juice*
> *Salt and pepper*
> *1 2-pound mackerel, cleaned and split for broiling*
> *Minced parsley or dill*

Combine butter, mustard, lemon juice, and salt and pepper to taste. Rub fish with this mixture and place on broiler rack, skin side down. (If broiling over charcoal, place skin side up.) Broil under hot flame for 5 minutes. Brush with remaining seasoning mixture and broil another 5 minutes, or until fish tests done. Sprinkle with parsley or dill. *Makes 2 servings.*

THE SEA AROUND US

Mackerel Baked in Beer

Of course I prefer the quality of fresh mackerel. But if you're really cut off and can't buy fresh mackerel, you can substitute a 1-pound can of mackerel, which costs only 25¢ in my market and will give you about the cheapest high-quality-protein dish possible. Just drain the can (strain the broth and use it in soup), remove any skin, divide each fish carefully in two, and remove the large back bones. As the fish is already well-cooked, baking time will be much reduced.

1 2-pound fresh mackerel, cleaned but left whole	¾ cup fish or chicken stock
1 teaspoon salt	¾ cup beer
½ teaspoon ground ginger	1 tablespoon butter
½ cup chopped scallions	1 tablespoon flour
2 peppercorns	1 teaspoon sugar

Rub the fish inside and out with salt and ginger. Fill cavity with scallions, place in ovenproof dish, and add peppercorns, stock and beer. Bake in 450° oven for ½ hour, or until fish tests done, basting every 5 minutes. Remove to hot platter, combine remaining ingredients and add to liquid, cook and stir until thickened. Pour over fish. *Makes 2 servings.*

Meg's Fish Dish

This dish was invented in my kitchen by a friend from abroad who stayed with me for a few days. I find it difficult to cook in someone else's kitchen, and one day when she asked to do the cooking I looked on in admiration, while making myself useful by finding the spoons and other equipment she needed. The cognac gives this dish a distinctive flavor, one that may mystify your guests.

2 pounds filets of sole or
    flounder
Salt
1 pound mushrooms,
    chopped fine
1 tablespoon olive oil
4 tablespoons butter

4 tablespoons flour
½ cup cream
4 tablespoons cognac
1½ cups fish stock or clam
    juice
Pepper
¼ cup grated Swiss cheese

Sprinkle fish lightly with salt and let stand 15 minutes. While filets are standing, sauté mushrooms briefly in the oil and 2 tablespoons of the butter. Sprinkle with 1 tablespoon of the flour, add the cream and stir until well blended. Add cognac and simmer for 5 minutes. Pour into baking dish. Rinse and dry the fish filets and lay them over the mushrooms in a flat, even layer. Combine remaining butter and flour, add stock and salt and pepper to taste, to make a white sauce. Pour over fish, sprinkle with cheese, and bake at 350° for 20 minutes. *Makes 8 servings.*

Mediterranean-American Lobster Tails

Our North Atlantic lobsters with their beautiful claws and sweet tender meat don't require any more elaborate preparation than boiling (or preferably steaming) and dipping in melted butter. Not that I don't like Lobster Thermidor and Lobster Newburg, Lobster a l'Américaine and Lobster Fra Diavolo—I do. Here is a sort of composite version of the last two, for you to make with the readily available frozen rock lobster tails. With its olive oil, tomatoes, and garlic, this is certainly a Mediterranean dish in origin, though now Americanized.

4 ½-pound rock lobster tails, or equivalent weight of smaller ones
6 tablespoons olive oil
2 small onions, chopped
2 cloves garlic, minced

2 cups Italian peeled tomatoes, drained
¼ teaspoon Tabasco sauce
1 teaspoon dried thyme
1 teaspoon dried tarragon
Salt and pepper
¼ cup cognac

Cut through the membrane on the underside of each lobster tail all the way to the end, but leave in shells. Sauté in hot oil until well colored Add onion and cook until translucent. Add next 5 ingredients, cover, and cook on low heat for 10 minutes. Add salt and pepper to taste. Flame dish with cognac and serve with something to help take up the sauce—rice, boiled potato, or French bread. *Makes 4 servings.*

Crab in Ale

1 pound fresh or canned crab meat	1 teaspoon caraway seeds
1 12-ounce bottle ale	2 tablespoons flour
1½ cups fish or chicken stock	2 tablespoons butter
1 small onion, minced	Salt and pepper
	Mace
	4 brioches or patty shells

Pick over crab meat carefully for cartilage. Heat ale and stock, add onion and caraway seeds, and simmer for 10 minutes. Pour off ½ cup of liquid and let cool. Mix with flour and butter and use to thicken remaining liquid. Add crab and heat through. Add salt and pepper to taste and a pinch of mace. Remove tops of brioches, tear out some of inside, fill with crab mixture, and replace top. The idea is not to get all the crab in the brioches; it will run down the sides as well. Use patty shells if you prefer, but the slight sweetening of the brioche dough goes well with the bitter taste of ale. *Makes 4 servings.*

Shrimp Boats

1½ pounds shrimps, shelled and de-veined, or frozen shrimps
½ cup butter
4 shallots, minced, or substitute scallions
2 tablespoons flour
1 cup fish stock, clam juice, or chicken bouillon
2 egg yolks
½ cup cream
Salt and pepper
4 small individual loaves of French bread, or rolls

If shrimps are larger than bite-sized, cut them in 2 or 3 pieces. Sauté in ¼ cup of the butter with shallots just until color of shrimp turns pink. Dissolve flour in stock and add to pan, stirring to prevent lumps, and simmer gently for 5 minutes. Mix egg yolks with cream and stir in gradually. Add salt and pepper to taste. Serve in prepared bread loaf, and if you're feeling particularly expansive, garnish with sliced black truffles briefly sautéed in butter. To prepare bread, cut in half lengthwise and hollow out each half, coat the cavities with the remaining ¼ cup butter, and put in a 325° oven for 20 minutes. You can also make a filling using scallops or mussels or a mixture of mollusks instead of shrimps. *Makes 4 servings.*

Shrimp and Artichoke Casserole

I think this recipe came into my collection from Adlai Stevenson, via *The New York Times*, and I like the convenience of its frozen ingredients when I'm in a hurry.

> 1 *package frozen artichoke hearts*
> 1 *pound frozen shrimps, shelled and de-veined*
> ¼ *pound mushrooms, sliced*
> 5 *tablespoons butter*
> 3 *tablespoons flour*
> 1½ *cups milk, cream, or stock (or any combination)*
> *Salt and pepper*
> ¼ *cup dry sherry*
> 1 *tablespoon* Worcestershire *sauce*
> ¼ *cup grated Swiss or Parmesan cheese*

Place frozen artichokes in ¼ cup boiling water, bring to second boil, simmer 5 minutes, and drain. Place frozen shrimps in salted boiling water to cover, bring to second boil, and drain immediately. Sauté mushrooms lightly in 2 tablespoons of the butter. Place artichokes, shrimps, and mushrooms in buttered casserole. Combine remaining butter, flour, and milk to make a white sauce; add salt and pepper to taste, plus sherry and Worcestershire sauce. Pour over ingredients in casserole, sprinkle with cheese, and bake for 20 minutes in 375° oven. *Makes 3 to 4 servings.*

Chicken Stuffed with Parsley

On a hot summer day in Noank, Connecticut, or any other place on earth, it's a good idea to cook a chicken on top of the stove instead of heating the oven. The method described here produces a juicy and tasty whole chicken. I usually stuff it with parsley but sometimes use other stuffings including fresh green grapes and cooked shrimps.

1 2½- to 3-pound chicken
Salt and pepper
5 tablespoons butter
½ cup chopped parsley
Chicken liver and gizzard, chopped

1 tablespoon olive oil
2 medium onions, sliced thinly
¾ cup chicken stock

Dry chicken carefully and sprinkle inside and outside with salt and pepper. Mix parsley with chicken liver and gizzards and 2 tablespoons softened butter. Stuff chicken and truss. Heat oil and remaining butter in casserole and brown chicken on all sides over medium heat for at least 10 minutes, turning with wooden spoons so you won't break the skin. Add onions and stock (or substitute dry vermouth or white wine), bring to boil, reduce heat, and cover partially with casserole lid or foil. Leave plenty of room for the steam to escape. Baste or turn the bird occasionally, watching to see if more liquid is needed, and cook gently until done, about 1 hour. (If desired, run under broiler to brown before serving.) The puréed onions make a good thick sauce. *Makes 4 servings.*

Chicken Breasts with Mushroom Stuffing

4 *tablespoons butter*
2 *tablespoons oil*
2 *tablespoons minced*
   green onions
2 *pounds mushrooms,*
   chopped fine
Salt

Cayenne pepper
2 *tablespoons* Madeira *or*
   sherry
1 *tablespoon chopped dill*
8 *half chicken breasts,*
   boned
½ *cup stock*

It takes a large pan to sauté 2 pounds of mushrooms. When butter and oil are very hot, add onions and mushrooms and cook for 5 minutes, stirring frequently. Season to taste with salt and cayenne. Add Madeira and dill, bring to high heat, and mix well. Open a small pocket on the inside of each half chicken breast and stuff in about 1 tablespoon of the mushroom mixture. Roll or fold over ends and place in a baking dish skin side up. Spread remaining stuffing over chicken and add stock. Bake covered at 325° for 1½ hours. Baste occasionally, adding more stock if needed. *Makes 8 servings.*

Chicken Casserole

During the many years I gave full time to my career I had to avoid all other time-consuming interests such as cooking. So I developed a very few specialties that I fixed over and over again. One of these is such a good stand-by that I still do it occasionally. Several friends have asked me for the recipe, and sometimes now when they invite me to dinner they say, "I hope you don't mind if I serve your chicken casserole." I don't mind at all, in fact I'm flattered. But one word of warning: don't serve a fine wine with this dish on account of the vinegar.

1 clove garlic, peeled and
   cut in half
4 tablespoons olive oil
1 small chicken, cut in
   serving pieces
½ lemon

Salt and pepper
4 tablespoons tarragon
   vinegar
½ teaspoon dried basil
1 bay leaf

In a casserole brown garlic in oil, remove and discard. Rub pieces of chicken with lemon, sprinkle with salt and pepper, and brown in oil. Add remaining ingredients, cover, and cook in 375° oven for 30 to 40 minutes, depending on size of chicken pieces. Serve with rice. *Makes 2 to 4 servings.*

Creamed Sweetbreads

Restaurants usually serve sweetbreads broiled or braised, but I like them better creamed—perhaps because I had them this way in my childhood. But I do think their flavor comes out best in cream sauce.

1 *pair sweetbreads*
3 *tablespoons butter*
3 *tablespoons flour*
1½ *cups stock or milk*
½ *cup Madeira or sherry*

Salt and white pepper
¼ *cup heavy cream*
2 *egg yolks*
½ *pound thinly sliced*
  mushrooms

Soak sweetbreads for 1 hour in cold water. Rinse, and put in kettle with water to cover and about 2 teaspoons salt for each quart of water. Bring to boil, then lift out, rinse with cold water, trim off any fat, and remove membranes. Return to kettle in which salted water has been kept at the boil, and simmer for 10 to 20 minutes depending on size of sweetbreads. They are done when firm to touch. Drain (reserve stock), let cool, and cut into ½" cubes. Combine 2 tablespoons of the butter with flour and stock, or if stock seems too salty to your taste, use milk. Simmer for 5 minutes, add wine, and salt and pepper to taste. Beat egg yolks into cream and add to sauce, together with sweetbreads. Sauté mushrooms in remaining 1 tablespoon butter and add. Heat through but do not boil. Serve in patty shells or on toast. *Makes 6 servings.*

Ginger Duck

This duck probably has Chinese ancestry, at least in the seasoning, but the cooking methods are American, and I feel it belongs to this part of the world rather than the Far East. Incidentally, it's as low in calories as any duck recipe can be.

1 frozen 4½-pound duck
¾ cup soy sauce
3 tablespoons ground ginger

Partly thaw the duck, enough to pry open the cavity, but pull or cut away as much fat as possible before it is completely thawed. (Peter learned in Greenland that it's much easier to cut meat and fat both when they're half frozen.) Rub duck with some of the soy sauce and ginger, and let stand until fully thawed. Place in deep casserole, add remaining soy sauce and ginger, add water to cover, and bring to boil. Reduce heat and simmer for 1 hour. Drain. (Liquid may be cooled, fat removed, and used to make duck soup.) Place on rack of roasting pan and roast in 450° oven for ½ hour or until crisp and done. *Makes 4 servings.*

Beef Stew with Red Wine

Because this dish is so often served at parties (and for good reasons) my recipe makes enough of it for 12 or more servings. If you don't have that many guests you can still make a large quantity and enjoy it again a day or two later. Since it is so popular, and there's a good chance some guests may have had it recently, I always choose an unusual appetizer and dessert to go with it.

6 *pounds lean beef, cut in 2" cubes*	1 *bay leaf, crumbled*
¾ *cup flour*	1 *tablespoon tomato paste*
½ *pound bacon, in one piece*	1 *bottle red wine*
Cooking oil	1¼ *cups beef bouillon, or more as required*
1 *teaspoon salt*	3 *pounds small white onions*
1 *teaspoon pepper*	6 *tablespoons butter*
2 *medium onions, sliced*	2 *teaspoons sugar*
2 *carrots, sliced thin*	1 *pound mushrooms*
3 *cloves garlic, chopped*	Parsley
¼ *teaspoon thyme*	

Roll cubes of meat in flour. Dice and parboil bacon. Heat 2 tablespoons oil in large skillet, brown bacon, and lift out with slotted spoon. Brown meat on all sides in fat remaining in skillet, and remove to large casserole. Sprinkle with salt and pepper. Brown sliced onions and carrots in skillet, adding more oil if needed. Add them to casserole, together with bacon, garlic, thyme, bay leaf, and tomato paste. Add wine and 1 cup bouillon. If you want a real Boeuf Bourgignonne use red Burgundy, the best you can afford. Wines of Bordeaux, California, and other places will make delicious stews, but the taste is different in each case. If the liquid does not cover the meat, add more bouillon. Bring to a simmer on top of stove, cover tightly, and bake at

350° for 3 hours. Meanwhile peel onions (peeling small onions is boring, but canned ones do not give the right taste) and brown them lightly in 2 tablespoons oil plus 2 tablespoons butter in a clean skillet. Sprinkle with sugar and shake the pan so that the onions get evenly glazed. Add ¼ cup bouillon, cover, and simmer for 10 minutes. Quarter or slice mushrooms and brown in 4 tablespoons butter. When meat is done, remove it from casserole and strain the sauce, skimming off fat. At this point you can adjust the amount of sauce by either boiling it down or adding more bouillon, and you can thicken it with *beurre manié*, if you like. For this much meat I like about 5 or 6 cups of sauce. Now everything can be combined and refrigerated until time for serving. To serve, heat meat, onions, and mushrooms in sauce to just below boiling point, sprinkle with chopped parsley, and serve with plain boiled potatoes or macaroni. *Makes 12 or more servings.*

Shrimp Curry

Just as my Ginger Duck isn't really Chinese, neither is this curry really Indian. But neither am I, and I find that this recipe makes a good dish, whatever it is. It was given to me by my friend, Ann. In place of shrimps I sometimes use other shellfish or boned chicken, and I like to make it for large buffet suppers because it can be cooked ahead, reheated, and eaten with only a fork.

1 pound shrimps	4 teaspoons Crosse &
2 tablespoons butter	Blackwell's curry powder
3 small onions, chopped	2 teaspoons ketchup
1 clove garlic, mashed	1 can cream of mushroom
1 small green pepper,	soup
chopped	1 can clear chicken broth
2 teaspoons Sunbrand Ma-	¾ cup milk
dras curry powder	Parsley

Cook shrimps for 3 minutes in lightly salted water, drain, peel, and de-vein. Sauté onions, garlic, green pepper, and curry powders in butter until onions are soft. Use only half the quantity of each curry powder if you prefer a mild dish. Add ketchup, soups, and milk, and simmer for 20 minutes. Add shrimps and heat through. Sprinkle with chopped parsley and serve with rice. *Makes 4 servings.*

Peter's Omelet

Peter sometimes shook his head when he watched me making omelets. I make them the traditional way, the way I used to watch Dione Lucas doing it when she had her restaurant on East 60th Street. I have a special omelet pan which is never used for anything else. And I get the filling ready in another pan, putting it in only when the omelet is folded onto the plate. Peter wondered, why not put everything in the pan together? Here is the way he did it.

2 *tablespoons butter*	*Salt and pepper*
2 *tomatoes, sliced*	1 *tablespoon chives*
6 *eggs, slightly beaten*	½ *pound Gruyere cheese,*
3 *tablespoons milk*	*cut in matchsticks*

Heat butter in large frying pan. Arrange tomato slices evenly in pan. Add milk to eggs and pour into pan, lifting tomatoes with spatula so that the eggs run underneath. Sprinkle with salt, pepper, and chives. Distribute the cheese over the top, especially in any spaces between the tomato slices, and cook on low fire until cheese begins to melt. Do not fold, but cut in pie-shaped quarters. *Makes 4 servings.*

Caviar Omelet

You probably have your own favorite way of making a plain omelet, and the idea here is either to fill it or garnish it with caviar and sour cream.

4 *eggs*
Pepper
Butter
1 *4-ounce jar caviar (Danish lumpfish or whatever you can afford)*
Sour cream

Beat eggs lightly and season with pepper but no salt because of heavily-salted caviar. Cook quickly in butter on a high fire, turning or folding as you like. Remove to hot platter, make a long slit in the top as though you were opening a baked potato to butter it, and spoon in the caviar. Serve with a dish of sour cream to be added in the amount each person wishes. *Makes 2 servings.*

Salmon Steaks in Aspic

4 individual-serving salmon steaks, fresh or frozen
1 cup dry white wine
3 cups fish stock, clam juice, or any delicate bouillon
1 egg white and shell
2 envelopes unflavored gelatin
Fresh tarragon or dill

Poach the salmon steaks in wine and stock until they are done. Remove any skin and bone that will come free without making them fall apart, and place them side by side on a platter with a small amount of space in between each steak. Strain bouillon and clarify it with egg white and shell. Dissolve gelatin in ½ cup cold water and mix with clarified bouillon. Cool until semi-congealed and spoon a thin film over fish steaks. Decorate each steak with leaves of tarragon or flattened sprigs of dill. Cover decorated fish carefully with a little more of the aspic. You can add any other decorations you like at this time—such as slices of hardboiled egg or olives—but I prefer aspics relatively plain. Chill in refrigerator until firm, spread on remaining aspic, and return platter to refrigerator until ready to serve. Any leftover aspic may be chopped and used as decoration. Mayonnaise is a traditional accompaniment, but don't use so much you drown the flavor of the aspic. *Makes 4 servings.*

Cold Salmon with Cucumber Dressing

Here is a dish in which you can perfectly well use canned salmon, though of course fresh poached salmon is fine for it too. Buy the best quality of red salmon you can find in a can.

1 1-pound can salmon
2 medium cucumbers
2 tablespoons lemon juice

1 carton (½ pint) plain yogurt
Watercress

Chill salmon, remove carefully from can, drain, discard any skin and bones, and arrange large chunks on 3 plates. Peel and seed cucumbers, dice, sprinkle with lemon juice, and let stand 15 minutes. Drain and combine with yogurt. Spread over salmon, and garnish plates generously with watercress. As canned salmon is often rather salty, the cucumber-yogurt sauce is deliberately left unsalted. *Makes 3 servings of less than 300 calories each.*

Shrimps in Tomato Aspic

This is an easy version. I've made the more complicated one too, but this works so well that I don't see any need to go to the extra trouble.

2 envelopes unflavored gelatin
1 cup dry vermouth
1 pound shrimps, cooked
4 12½-ounce cans madrilene soup

2 cups sour cream
1 tablespoon tarragon vinegar, or to taste
2 teaspoons sugar, or to taste

Soften gelatin in ½ cup of the vermouth. Bring contents of 1 can of soup to boil, pour over gelatin mixture, and stir to dissolve. Stir in remaining vermouth and soup. Cover bottom of an 8-cup ring mold with ½ cup of mixture and chill until almost set. Arrange shrimps in neat row around bottom of mold and spoon soup mixture over them carefully. Chill again, and when set add rest of soup. Chill 8 hours. Unmold and serve with sour cream whipped with vinegar and sugar to taste. *Makes about 10 servings.*

Lobster Salad

This is another dish you can prepare with frozen rock lobster tails, or even with canned lobster, though fresh lobster meat from your fish market or picked out of the shells of lobsters you've simmered at home yourself will be even better.

1 *pound cooked lobster*
   meat
½ *pound mushrooms*
2 *medium cucumbers*
Salt
1 *large green pepper*

1 *large avocado*
Lemon juice
1 *tablespoon capers*
½ *cup vinaigrette sauce*
1 *hardboiled egg*

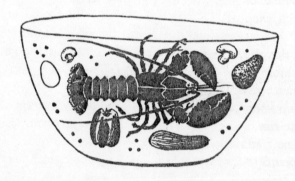

Cut lobster in bite-sized pieces. Wash mushrooms. If they are very small, leave them whole; if medium, slice them; if large, remove stems and cut caps bite size. In any case, they are eaten raw. Peel and seed cucumbers, cut bite size, sprinkle with salt, let stand 15 minutes, then drain. Chop green pepper rather fine. Cut avocado bite size and sprinkle with lemon juice. Now mix capers and crumbled yolk of egg into vinaigrette. Dice egg white. Combine all ingredients except avocado and toss well. Add avocado, taking care not to mash or break it. Refrigerate for at least 1 hour. Turn salad once more very carefully just before serving. *Makes 4 servings.*

Rice Salad with Buried Treasures

The name implies that this is a rich or fancy dish. Quite the contrary, it is simple to make and it uses some of the cheapest fish that come in cans.

6 cups cold cooked rice
1 cup tarragon vinegar
Any or all of the following:
  1 can salmon
  1 can sardines
  1 can anchovies
  1 can minced or whole clams
½ pound oil-cured black olives
½ cup chopped scallions

Mix rice and vinegar. Drain all cans of fish, putting aside water or broth, but adding oil to rice. Remove skin and bones from salmon, remove bones from sardines (if they are large enough to matter), and chop up anchovies. Add fish, olives, and scallions to rice, and mix. If rice is still dry enough to absorb it, you may now add liquid drained from fish. Chill for at least 1 hour. *Makes 6 to 8 servings.*

Green Pilaf

2 *tablespoons oil*	1 *cup rice*
1 *cup chopped spinach*	2½ *cups chicken stock*
½ *cup chopped parsley*	*Salt and pepper*
½ *cup chopped green onion stems*	

Sauté all chopped greens in oil for 5 minutes. Add rice, stir and sauté for another 5 minutes. Bring stock to boil and add to rice. Add pepper and salt to taste; if you use canned chicken broth remember it may be well salted. Cover and simmer for 25 minutes or until rice is tender. Drain any unabsorbed liquid. This pilaf can be served hot or cold, loose or in a mold. It goes well with fish, chicken, or veal. If you want to serve it cold as a rice salad, mix in ½ cup vinaigrette. *Makes about 4 cups.* You can make any number of variations: For red pilaf instead of green, substitute chopped peeled tomatoes for greens and 1 cup tomato juice for 1 cup of the chicken stock. I've made magenta rice with beet juice and of course yellow rice with saffron. I've never tried to make blue rice, but it ought to be possible with blueberries or grape juice. And black rice with the ink from a cuttlefish . . . ? But I don't think these last two would taste nearly so good as green rice.

Beets with Greens

Why should anybody take the trouble to cook fresh beets when the canned ones are perfectly good in salads (especially with Belgian endive and vinaigrette dressing), or pickled, or served hot with melted butter? One reason is to get the greens. "Anybody want these beet tops?" said the man at my vegetable store one day as he tore them off and wrapped the roots for an unsophisticated customer. This wouldn't happen in an Italian neighborhood, where beet greens all by themselves (actually a different variety) are an expensive delicacy. They need nothing more than quick cooking like spinach, and seasoning with salt and lemon juice (plus a touch of olive oil or butter if you like). Where you have only the tops that come with a bunch of beets—they have to be fresh and crisp, of course, not withered or yellow—you can extend their quantity with diced beets.

>   *1 bunch beets with greens (about 8 small beets)*
>   *1½ teaspoons salt*
>   *2 wedges lemon*

Cook beets and greens separately; the beets, washed but unpeeled, in water to cover with 1 teaspoon salt until tender; the greens, stems removed, coarsely chopped, in minimum water with ½ teaspoon salt, just until tender. Peel and dice half of beets and add to greens. (Put other half aside for another use.) Serve with lemon wedges and a dribble of melted butter or olive oil if desired. *Makes 2 servings.*

Pickled Beets

This is a good way to use up the beets you put aside in the last recipe, though when you take the trouble to make pickled beets you might want to make enough to last a while. They'll keep in the refrigerator (in a covered jar) for a couple of weeks.

>   *2 bunches beets, cooked, peeled, and sliced*
>   *1 cup vinegar*
>   *½ cup sugar*
>   *1 tablespoon pickling spices, tied in cheesecloth*

Combine all ingredients and simmer for 5 minutes. Let cool, then discard spices. Serve either hot or cold. Some people like a sliced onion in with the beets. If you add cornstarch and butter to the liquid and serve hot, they become Harvard beets. *Makes 6 servings, or more as a pickle.*

Johnnycake

Cornbread, spoonbread, hoecake, johnnycake—by whatever name, and whether baked in an oven or on a griddle, these cornmeal breads seem to go well with many American foods, especially seafood. I like the following version because it makes a kind of *crepe* that you can eat with butter as you would a square of cornbread, or with a filling of creamed mussels, scallops, etc., or with a sweet filling for dessert. You can even wrap them up in foil and take them along to eat on a picnic, as the name suggests—it is supposed to have been originally "journey cake."

    2 *cups cornmeal*   *½ cup milk*
    1 *teaspoon salt*   *¼ cup melted butter*
    2 *tablespoons molasses*

    Boil up 2 cups of water and stir it into the cornmeal. Add other ingredients. Cook batter on griddle in pancakes about 5" across. *Makes 6 servings.*

Coffee Jelly with Stonington Cream

If you like the sauce for this dessert as well as my friends in Stonington, Connecticut do (they invented it), then you may take to eating or drinking it by itself, or with macaroons.

3 tablespoons unflavored
  powdered gelatin
3 cups boiling hot coffee
½ cup sugar, plus sugar to
  sprinkle mold

½ cup medium dry sherry
1 pint coffee ice cream
2 tablespoons gin or vodka

Soften gelatin in ½ cup cold water and dissolve in hot coffee. Stir in sugar and sherry. Rinse a 1-quart ring mold with water, sprinkle with sugar, and shake out excess. Pour coffee mixture into mold and chill for at least 4 hours. Unmold and serve with either Stonington Cream or whipped cream. To make Stonington Cream, place ice cream and gin or vodka in blender and blend until smooth. Serve immediately. *Makes 6 servings.*

Beach Plum Jam

Beach plums grow wild in the dunes between Easthampton and Montauk, Long Island, and many other places. Their flavor is entirely different from other plums, resembling an extra-tart combination of cherries, grapes, and plums. Too sour to eat raw, they make a wonderful preserve. Last year I helped a friend pick some, and at Christmas he gave me several jars of delicious jam made only with the addition of sugar. The following recipe adds some optional spices.

To make beach plum pulp, wash the fruit, remove stems, and cook in just the water that clings to the plums. When fruit is soft, remove and discard pits.

4 cups beach plum pulp
3 to 4 cups sugar, according to taste
4 tablespoons lemon juice or cider vinegar, optional
1½ teaspoons ground cloves, optional
1½ teaspoons ground cinnamon, optional

Combine all ingredients (use the smaller amount of sugar, adding the other cup at the end if you want it), bring to boil, stir, and simmer ½ hour. Pour into sterilized jars and seal.

Deep-Dish Apple Pie

You probably have your own recipe for a good deep-dish apple pie with cinnamon and nutmeg, so here is a more unusual one with almonds, lemon, and rum.

1½ cups flour	5 large apples, sliced
½ teaspoon salt	1 cup brown sugar
¾ cup butter	1 lemon
¼ cup ground almonds	¼ cup dark Jamaica rum

Sift flour and salt, and cut in ½ cup cold butter. Mix in almonds and cold water, enough to make a stiff dough. Refrigerate. Combine remaining ¼ cup butter, melted, with apples, sugar, and juice and grated rind of lemon. Put in greased baking dish and cover with chilled pastry rolled out to fit. Seal pastry against sides, but cut decorative holes in center. Bake at 450° for 15 minutes, then at 325° for 25 minutes more or until apples test done. After removing from oven add rum carefully through holes in crust, using an eye dropper, basting syringe, or small funnel. *Makes 6 servings.*

Index